Dog Park Design, Development, and Operation

Marilynn R. Glasser

EdD, CPRP, CPSI

Human Kinetics

Library of Congress Cataloging-in-Publication Data

Glasser, Marilynn R., 1949-
  Dog park design, development, and operation / Marilynn R. Glasser, EdD.
    pages cm
  Includes bibliographical references and index.
  1. Parks for dogs. I. Title.
  SF427.45.G53 2013
  636.7'0835--dc23

                          2012050264

ISBN-10: 0-7360-9155-6 (print)
ISBN-13: 978-0-7360-9155-8 (print)

Acquisitions Editor: Gayle Kassing, PhD; **Developmental Editor:** Jacqueline Eaton Blakley; **Assistant Editor:** Anne Rumery; **Copyeditor:** Joy Wotherspoon; **Indexer:** Andrea Hepner; **Permissions Manager:** Dalene Reeder; **Graphic Designer:** Nancy Rasmus; **Graphic Artist:** Kathleen Boudreau-Fuoss; **Cover Designer:** Keith Blomberg; **Photographs (cover):** Background photo, Marilynn R. Glasser; bottom left, Nora VandenBerghe; bottom right and top right, Kathleen Burleson; **Photographs (interior):** Photo on page v, George Peters/iStockphoto; photo on page 1, Walter Arce I Dreamstime.com; photo on page 3, Ronnie Kaufman/Lithium/age fotostock; photo on page 9, Rob Van Esch I Dreamstime.com; photo on page 61, James Boardman I Dreamstime.com; photo on page 69, MachineHeadz/iStockphoto; photo on page 87, I4lcocl2 I Dreamstime.com; photo on page 99, Ricardo De Mattos/ iStockphoto; photo on page 117, Leung Cho Pan I Dreamstime.com; photo on page 121, JUNIORS BILDARCHIV/ age fotostock; photo on page 122, Julie Feinstein I Dreamstime.com; photos on pages 12, 13, 21, 23, 25, 27 (top), 28, 30, 32, 35, 38, 42-47, 49, 51-53 (left), 54 (bottom), 55-58 (top), 63-65, 72, 74, 76, 78, 79, 91, 93-97, 100, 102 (bottom), 105, 106, and 109, courtesy of Marilynn R. Glasser; photos on pages 5, 6, 17, 19, 27 (bottom), 54 (top), 58 (bottom), 81, 83, 89, 102 (top), 104, and 119, courtesy of Kathleen Burleson; photos on pages 53 (right) and 103, courtesy of Marianne Proctor; all others © Human Kinetics, unless otherwise noted; **Art Manager:** Kelly Hendren; **Associate Art Manager:** Alan L. Wilborn; **Printer:** Edwards Brothers Malloy

Printed in the United States of America   10   9   8   7   6   5   4   3   2   1

The paper in this book is certified under a sustainable forestry program.

Human Kinetics
Website: www.HumanKinetics.com

United States: Human Kinetics
P.O. Box 5076
Champaign, IL 61825-5076
800-747-4457
e-mail: humank@hkusa.com

Canada: Human Kinetics
475 Devonshire Road Unit 100
Windsor, ON N8Y 2L5
800-465-7301 (in Canada only)
e-mail: info@hkcanada.com

Europe: Human Kinetics
107 Bradford Road
Stanningley
Leeds LS28 6AT, United Kingdom
+44 (0) 113 255 5665
e-mail: hk@hkeurope.com

Australia: Human Kinetics
57A Price Avenue
Lower Mitcham, South Australia 5062
08 8372 0999
e-mail: info@hkaustralia.com

New Zealand: Human Kinetics
P.O. Box 80
Torrens Park, South Australia 5062
0800 222 062
e-mail: info@hknewzealand.com

E5104

This book is dedicated to Linda Trepel-Cantor, my inspiration, my friend, and a wonderful dog park advocate and visionary who left us far too soon.

From the day Linda first came to me to inquire about developing a dog park, her passion and enthusiasm were obvious and infectious. As an amazing can-do person, she led folks through a barrage of naysayers, which culminated in an attractive municipal dog park. The politics and obstacles she encountered for nearly five years were a Herculean challenge, but the dog park she championed speaks volumes about this special woman's tenacity and determination.

Linda's heartfelt, positive attitude about the many benefits of a community dog park had a huge effect on me as a parks professional. She enabled me to realize how much I wanted to be responsive to a community's needs and desires when it came to residents' beloved dogs.

Though Linda passed away shortly after I was asked to write this book, I was thrilled to be able to tell her about it. It is truly a most fitting tribute, and my great joy, to dedicate *Dog Park Design, Development, and Operation* to this special lady whom I miss so much.

Contents

1 Why Build a Dog Park?   1

Our dogs are *so* important to us. Dog parks provide a unique opportunity for a community's many dog owners to recreate in a safe, enjoyable outdoor environment with their friends—both canine and human!

2 Making the Case   9

No matter how excited you are about a dog park, you can be sure that some people will not share the enthusiasm. With patience and positive education, you can address concerns and highlight the advantages of the planned park!

3 Planning   21

Let's get the dog park started! You'll need to garner support, select a site, and much more.

4 Components   35

How does a space become a dog park? Find out which components you need to build your dog park right!

5 Landscaping and Maintenance   61

Little effort is needed to keep the dog park in good shape. Find out how to maximize your park's aesthetics and appeal, making it attractive and user friendly for all!

6 Dog Park Rules and Etiquette   69

Your dog park will bring together all kinds of people and dogs in one place! Learn how to establish rules and guidelines that will bring out the best behavior in everyone.

Preface

In parks throughout North America, facilities like playgrounds, soccer fields, and picnic areas are more than commonplace—they are expected, desirable components of our community parks. The addition of off-leash enclosures for dog owners to enjoy with their pets is a relatively new concept that has become an increasingly popular park feature. I believe that dog parks, too, will soon become an expected and appreciated staple of public parks.

So it is imperative that a professional guide, presenting a best-practices perspective, be made available to park professionals and others interested in creating these facilities. This book fulfills that need. Thus, those interested in creating a high-quality dog park will be equipped with all the required information, from concept to completion and beyond. This book explains and presents the steps in creating a professional-quality off-leash facility, including important related topics, such as location, community benefits, maintenance, design, amenities, rules, and even programming for the completed dog park facility. Whether it is to be developed in an existing park or as a new stand-alone facility, this book provides a straightforward approach and process to creating a wonderful community dog park.

Though there have been several books and pamphlets published about dog parks, this one focuses specifically on the development of dog parks from the perspective of the parks, recreation, and leisure services profession. Thus, you obtain appropriate, comprehensive guidance to enable the creation of a professional, high-quality park facility that reflects proven park standards and techniques relating to such topics as the natural environment and resources, landscape, maintenance, and community needs.

This book offers proven information about creating high-quality dog park facilities. Since these facilities are still often considered relatively new, many of the entities looking to create dog parks simply search the Internet or try to locate and contact places that have already developed dog parks. Though information is certainly available online, much of it might be dated; it might apply only to specific geographic areas; and, of course, it cannot respond to individual sites, circumstances, and problems, which are usually plentiful. Contacting others who have already developed dog parks increases the opportunity for repeating mistakes and problems—both long and short term. Thus, this book puts the needed information in perspective, as a guide, addressing both the general concerns and many common specific issues that are often a part of the process.

The audience for this book includes a variety of people and groups. First, certainly park and recreation professionals would benefit from using this book as an instructional manual. Since this is my background, I cover many of the pluses and minuses that need to be addressed from this venue. Additional professionals who will find this book helpful include municipal and park planners, landscape architects, and community developers. More private, commercial groups could include development professionals and contractors. Homeowners associations and the like might also use the book. Both dog lovers and canine professionals would find the book helpful, and they are often among the first in a community to initiate interest in developing a dog park. Finally, forward-thinking people in the hotel and tourism industries might find the book a beneficial guide to developing high-quality off-leash facilities for their guests' pets, especially since pet-friendly accommodations are gaining popularity.

You will be able to easily understand, address, follow, and implement the various steps presented. Though the material is aimed at park professionals, laypeople should also be able to use the information with the assistance and guidance of a professional.

Dog Park Design, Development, and Operation is arranged in the natural order in which most community development projects evolve and progress. Chapter 1 begins with a discussion of the popularity of pet ownership, with eye-opening statistics about how devoted people are to their dogs. That devotion translates into the interest and passion that dog owners express when first hearing of, seeing, or experiencing a dog park. The typical enthusiastic reaction is that they want one in *their* neighborhood! Dog park terms are then defined, and some general park terminology is identified. Finally, we consider how dog parks naturally appeal to a populace eager for fun and recreation with their dogs.

Chapter 2 discusses the typical scenarios and challenges that communities experience in the initial phases of dog park development. The benefits and value of a dog park must be understood, appreciated, and communicated to attract needed support. It presents ways to handle and defuse some of the adversarial issues that often arise as a community explores the feasibility and advantages of a dog park. Education, especially in communities new to the dog park concept, is key.

Following the initial stages of dog park development, planning objectives are determined. Chapter 3 discusses development concerns, as well as variables related to the proposed sites and design. The pluses and minuses of location options must be carefully identified and weighed as plans are developed.

Chapter 4 identifies and explains the components and amenities for dog parks, including the required signage. Some components will be described as essential, others as optional. Safety of people and dogs is always a priority, and it must be taken into consideration when developing a dog park.

Though both are quite minimal, the maintenance and landscaping needs for a dog park are described in chapter 5. The importance of input from parks maintenance employees in a dog park's development and design is discussed, since they will play an important role in the operation of the new facility. Specific needs and suggested tasks are explained and are considered essential to a high-quality dog park. Regional differences, especially climate, can affect maintenance concerns, and they must be considered and reflected in the planning.

The actual operation of a dog park, to a large extent, is a function of the rules the public is expected to follow, since a dog park is a self-policed facility. Chapter 6 concerns the all-important dog park rules as well as dog park etiquette. The fact that dog parks are as popular as they are (again, through self-policing) means, for the most part, that dog parks work! Rules are identified and explained. It is in *everyone's* best interests that rules be adhered to and supported by the users. Dog park etiquette is another important factor for dog park operations. It primarily refers to *human* behaviors that can help maximize the dog park experience. This type of information, going beyond the dog park rules, can be a helpful bonus for all dog park users—dogs *and* their owners.

When a dog park is completed, it should be treated as any new park facility, with a celebratory, festive grand opening! Chapter 7 suggests a variety of features, activities, exhibits, and positive media coverage that can be included to commemorate both the culmination of hard work and the inception of a wonderful new community park facility.

Evaluation, covered in chapter 8, is an essential aspect of any park or recreation endeavor. Recommended categories and questions to be included in a comprehensive evaluative procedure are identified and explained. Park administrators should observe and document usage patterns, adherence to rules, problems of any type, and users' comments, concerns, and suggestions. This evaluation step helps ensure that a community dog park will become everything the supporters hoped for, expected, and envisioned.

Chapter 9 discusses marketing and programming for the new dog park. Park professionals should understand the importance of marketing the community's new facility to ensure all residents know of its existence and the opportunities it presents for enhancement of quality of life for residents with and without dogs. Fun, family-oriented programs and events, usually dog related, of course, enhance what virtually always becomes a very popular new community venue.

In a comprehensive, understandable manner, this book shows how to develop a high-quality dog park facility that dog owners will happily use, appreciate, and truly enjoy. Using this text will reduce the possibility of overlooking any of the required steps in the development process. The guesswork for creating a dog park facility, especially for those perhaps only minimally familiar with the concept, is removed in this text. As one devotedly passionate about dog parks, I have endeavored to offer my knowledge, experience, and enthusiasm to make the process of developing a dog park successful and rewarding.

Finally, throughout the book, brief descriptions and stories of my experiences visiting dog parks throughout the country should provide some additional color as you proceed through the text. These experiences include discussions, meetings, comments, and encounters, some with a comical flavor, others clearly exhibiting the importance of following tried and true methods along with the best practices indicated throughout the book. Thus, in addition to the information, you will find these descriptions and stories poignant, interesting, and helpful.

So now, I'll ask you to *come, stay, sit,* read, and enjoy!

Acknowledgments

First, I must thank the patient Human Kinetics folks who waded through this process with me as a newbie author. Gayle Kassing and Jackie Blakley were downright inspiring in demystifying the publishing steps as well as holding my hand through the computer! They answered my silly questions, repeatedly explained the procedures, and, more often than not, gave me extra time with the deadlines. Yet they also made me feel professional and knowledgeable throughout. I am so grateful to them; they should win some sort of huge award for the kindness and understanding they showed me. I am very proud of the final project; it is indeed everything we believed it would be. Again, sincere thanks.

My aunt Dorothy Lamb, who passed away during the writing of the book, was my first influence in becoming a true lover of animals, nature, and pets. She made me realize the depth of our capacity to love all creatures and, in turn, their capacity to return that love many times over as well as to trust and depend on us, unconditionally, forever. I thank her for enabling me to realize how lucky we are to have pets in our lives. I also thank her for sharing her wonderful, caring, and compassionate feelings for the world's creatures and passing it on to me and others fortunate enough to have known her and been touched by her wisdom about pets and all animals that bring joy to our lives. She was a very special inspiration to me as well as a fun, caring, and important presence throughout my life. I loved her very much, miss her, and cherish my memories of her every day. She joined me for my very earliest dog park visits and would have been so pleased with this book!

Thanks to my friend and colleague Kathleen Burleson for many of the photographs throughout the book, primarily the *best* ones. Her willingness to schlep to dog parks with me, sometimes in not-so-great weather, is greatly appreciated. Her enthusiasm for getting shots of precisely what I wanted and needed took patience and timing—and I am certainly grateful that she aimed to please and truly hit the target over and over again!

I must also thank my dear friend and colleague Kathleen Gately. For many years, when we attended the National Recreation and Park Association annual congresses together, she joined me on my many dog park explorations and picture-taking endeavors, the results of which appear throughout this book. She helped me locate parks all over the country (*without* a GPS), and I certainly appreciated her professional camaraderie on those treks. Her patience with me on the trips is legendary, especially when some of the dog parks were particularly tough to find. I so appreciated her assistance and kindness—especially when I was frustrated!

I was lucky to have a student assist me as part of an honors project at Lehman College in the Bronx, New York, where I'm an adjunct assistant professor. Jennifer Giusti, now a full-time recreation and parks professional, was a terrific help to me and conducted research with passion and efficiency that I greatly appreciate. She accompanied me on several community visits relating to dog parks and participated in client meetings. She quickly grasped the meaningfulness of these facilities and their importance to the dog-owning public. I am grateful for her enthusiasm and her assistance with this book.

A terrific graphic artist, author, and friend, Doris Tomaselli, drew the wonderful dog park in chapter 4. I love the whimsical flavor she brought to the picture, and I especially appreciate her willingness to tweak her work many times to create just what I wanted. I must certainly thank her and mention that her patience was particularly noteworthy because, as the picture evolved, I was so excited about it that I kept requesting additions! The finished product is just fabulous.

Richard Zenk is my landscaper; my go-to guy about plants, outdoor maintenance, drainage, and an assortment of other grounds-related issues; and a great friend. I came to him with questions, especially the more technical ones, and he was always immensely helpful. I must thank RZ for his time and patience and for always making sure I got it.

Throughout the writing of this book, I looked forward to my daily bagel and coffee from Tom-Tom's Bagel Café just down the street from my office. The Tom-Tom's crew was always welcoming and supportive, and I enjoyed rewarding myself in this fashion. I appreciate their smiles, kindness, and especially, as their motto says, "The best damn bagels. Period."

Finally, my Marianne has graciously endured this lengthy ordeal with me. She has been there for me every step of the way, even when some of the steps were particularly challenging. Always supportive, caring, and helpful, she was always so reassuring and important to me. Knowing that I was a novice but driven to do a great job, I could always count on her for feedback when I'd ask, "Can I run something by you?" I thank her from the bottom of my heart for her time, interest, patience, and love.

I learned about the joys of sharing life with dogs through my own—Gin, Ferron, Sascha, Moxie, Mabel, and now our new young ones, Sadie and Stella. They all touch my heart and soul, and I will be better for having had them in my life. I love them all.

Building a Dog Park: An Overview

The following provides an overview of the various tasks needed to create a quality community dog park. They are in a semblance of order, but, from one community to another, or under a variety of other circumstances, the order must be considered flexible and variable. Indeed, in some municipalities, tasks may be required that are not mentioned here; every community is unique and has its own cast of characters, many of whom often make themselves known when a dog park may be on the horizon. This community uniqueness, whether reflecting support or opposition, must be recognized and appreciated. In whatever order, the following steps describe the required basics for creating a professionally constructed dog park.

- Interested parties come forward. If the idea is initiated by people outside the municipal parks agency, those administration professionals should be contacted and become involved (input from parks maintenance personnel and an animal control officer should be sought early on).

- Appropriate research about developing dog parks, dog ownership, and the community benefits of dog parks should be conducted by both the supporters and park professionals.

- Contact government officials and politicians to make them aware of the interest and support for a community dog park.

- Begin publicity to develop additional awareness of the interest in developing a dog park and to increase community support. Plan to conduct community informational presentations.

- Learn about the likely arguments individuals opposing the proposed dog park project will have and questions they will ask. Be prepared with appropriate responses that will allay fears and concerns.

- Ascertain and fulfill any municipal requirements for approval to move forward.

- Consider possible site locations with appropriate topography, accessibility, access to water for fountains, proximity to other park venues (if site is in an existing park) and neighbors, and ease of supervision and maintenance. Final site selection should be determined with assistance from municipal park professionals.

- With municipal assistance, including parks maintenance personnel, determine all necessary plans and related funding needs for the new dog park facility: design layout, fencing, surfacing needs, parking, amenities, and so on.

- Determine the construction and installation needs as well as specific necessary amenities and municipal procedures (e.g., formal or informal bidding requirements).

- Determine how the needed funds can be obtained, such as municipal funding, possible grant funding, private and commercial donations, fundraising, and so on. Also determine if services, equipment, or supplies may be donated.

- Develop a schedule for all needed work, including purchasing, obtaining, constructing, and installing all equipment for the dog park, such as parking, property clearing, fencing and gates, ADA compliance, surfacing type, hardscape surfaces, water fountains, waste cans, waste bag stations, benches, shade structures, signage, landscaping, and so on.

- Determine dog park rules and etiquette for publication and signage.

- At some point, the dog park should be named. Sometimes naming the new dog park can be accomplished through a community contest, adding interest and support for the facility. This could also be conducted as a fundraising event.

- Explore, consider, and develop potential program and event opportunities using the dog park.

- Develop marketing strategies for encouraging use of the dog park. If possible, an artistic supporter may be instrumental in developing graphics or a logo for the new dog park. The artwork can then be used for publicity and signage developing helpful visual recognition for the dog park which can assist and encourage support.

- Construct the dog park. Clear property (as needed); identify and prepare parking areas; erect fencing and gates; pave and install hard surface areas and water fountains; site and place (preferably in a secure or permanent manner) waste cans, waste bag stations, shade structures, benches, and signs; landscape (usually minimal).

- Periodically publicize the progress of the dog park project to build additional support, positive anticipation, excitement, and enthusiasm.

- Conduct a gala grand opening day for the new dog park. Components to be considered may include informational handouts, media attendance and participation, music, formal presentations, dog parade and contests, refreshments, informational booths sponsored by local vendors and community organizations, and educational demonstrations.

- After a period of time, evaluate the facility (e.g., how it's operating, community reactions and usage, maintenance) as well as the related new programming and events.

Why Build a Dog Park?

Our dogs are *so* important to us. Dog parks provide a unique opportunity for a community's many dog owners to recreate in a safe, enjoyable outdoor environment with their friends—both canine and human!

We love our dogs! They are members of our families, special four-legged friends who ask little more than nourishment and attention as, in turn, they give us years of joy and companionship and contribute wonderfully to our quality of life. This first chapter begins with some of the fascinating current statistics reflecting the passion of dog owners as well as some general facts and information on pet travel and the financial aspects and health benefits of dog ownership. Since some dog park terms have several meanings and may vary from one region to another, *dog park* and various related terms are defined so you understand the terminology throughout the book.

Our Passion for Pets

Clearly, our passion for our dogs has created interest in dog parks and made their development popular. Requesting facilities for recreational enjoyment with our beloved pets truly makes sense and is totally understandable!

In the United States, more households have pets than have children. Over 75 million dogs are owned in the United States (ASPCA, 2009), which is the highest dog population in the world (Lederer, 2009a), and 39 percent of U.S. households own at least one dog (Humane Society of the United States, 2008). Of these, 63 percent own one dog, 25 percent own two dogs, and 12 percent own three or more dogs (Humane Society of the United States, 2008). Based on recent surveys conducted in 20 of the world's major nations, the United States has the highest percentage of dogs and cats (American Humane Association, 2013). Brazil and China have the next-highest percentages.

We spend plenty of money on our beloved pets! Whether we're referring to food, bedding, toys, treats, health, clothing, or even day care, pets are big business. The pet market is the second fastest-growing retail industry (behind consumer electronics) (Wolfe, 2009). Each year, Americans spend more than $43 billion on pets, including $8 billion on dog food and $4 billion on cat food, more than they spend on baby food (Lederer, 2009a). In 2007, pet owners spent double the amount they spent on their pets in 1997 (Wolfe, 2009).

Of course, people have good reasons for devoting so much money to the care of their pets. Studies have been around for some time showing numerous health benefits for pet owners. In addition, for those who do not (or cannot) have pets, such as nursing home residents, opportunities for pet therapy are ever increasing in a variety of health care settings. Our pets mean a great deal to us, and research continues to show that they help keep us healthy! Proven benefits include the following (Cat Channel, 2009):

- Reduced risk of cardiovascular disease
- Higher survival rates from heart attack
- Significantly lower use of general practitioner services
- Better physical and psychological well-being for seniors

Pet Partners (formerly the Delta Society), a human services organization dedicated to improving people's health and well-being through interactions with animals, found no significant social or economic difference between

Pets are increasingly used in therapeutic settings because their companionship has proven health benefits.

people who do or do not have a pet that adequately explains the differences in health outcomes, leading to the conclusion that pet ownership itself is the primary cause of the positive benefits. Lawrence Norvell, president and CEO of Pet Partners, said, "At a time in which our society is looking for treatment alternatives to complement Western medicine, research is constantly demonstrating that pets can have a profound impact on people's physical and emotional health. We are excited to see more health care professionals and other leaders embracing the fact that pets can be a cost-effective approach to improving people's health while enriching their lives" (Cat Channel, 2009).

You might be surprised to find that these positive and healthy feelings about our pets can be quantified. They contribute to our lives in so many ways! Nine out of ten pet owners say they consider their pet a member of the family (American Humane Association, 2013). They treat them that way at holidays, according to Richard Lederer, author of *A Treasury for Dog Lovers*, giving them Christmas presents (63%) to the tune of about $5 billion a year, hanging Christmas stockings (40%), signing their pets' names on greeting cards (25%), and including news about their pets in their holiday cards (64%) (2009a). About 27 percent of pet owners have taken their pet to a professional photographer to have pictures taken with family, Santa, or the Easter Bunny, and 58 percent include pets in family and holiday portraits. Thirty-six percent of dog owners give presents for their pets' birthdays.

We love to travel with our pets! An estimated 29.1 million Americans say they have traveled with a pet in the past three years. We are seeing more and more pet-friendly accommodations (the American Automobile Association even publishes a guide), various types of pet carriers and safety-related travel items for pets, travel services for pets and their owners, and even pet-oriented vacation programs. The days of no pets allowed may be numbered. The travel industry has been changing the rules and accommodations to attract families traveling with pets. New programs are also available for enjoying time away from home with pets, such as walking and hiking tours. A new pet passport even allows animals to travel easily between participating countries without quarantine (Guerrero, 2009). Companion animals commonly take day trips, weekend excursions, and family vacations, and they comprise a fast-growing segment of the industry (Guerrero, 2009).

Consider these other bits of evidence of our passion for our pets:

- About 37 percent of dog owners have their pets' picture prominently displayed in their homes, and 14 percent display it at their place of work. Approximately 10 percent of pet owners carry their pets' picture in their wallet or purse (American Humane Association, 2013).

- In about 20 percent of pet households, the TV, radio, or stereo is left on while the pets are alone at home, presumably so they don't get lonely (American Humane Association, 2013).

- Sixteen percent of dog owners have bought a home or car with a pet in mind (American Humane Association, 2013).

- In 40 percent of pet households, dogs are allowed to lie on the furniture. Thirty-nine percent of dogs are permitted to sleep at night on a family member's bed, and 45 percent of pet owners set up a special bed for their pets in the home (American Humane Association, 2013).

- Twenty-five percent of pet owners blow dry their pets' hair after a bath (American Humane Association, 2013).

- When a pet dies, 58 percent of pet owners bury the pet on their property (American Humane Association, 2013).

- More than 90 percent of people surveyed, including those who don't own pets, felt the following groups could lead more satisfying lives if they had a dog or cat companion: people living alone, senior citizens, people with disabilities, and young children (American Humane Association, 2013).

- Thirty-three percent of dog owners talk to their dogs on the phone and leave answering machine messages for them while away (Lederer, 2009a).

- An estimated one million dogs in America have been named as primary beneficiaries in their owners' wills (Lederer, 2009a).

Again, we indeed love our dogs! We share our lives, our homes, our families, and our lifestyles with them. As Richard Lederer, a California-based author of more than 30 books on language, humor, and history, lovingly wrote in his introduction to *A Treasury for Dog Lovers,* "The partnership is unique in inter-species relationships. The loyalty and devotion that dogs demon-strate as part of their natural pack-animal instincts exempli-fies the human idea of love and friendship. Dogs seem to view their humans as members of their pack, and the same goes for most dog owners. To us, dogs are adopted sons and daughters who are short, hairy, walk on all fours, and possess rudimentary speech" (2009b, p. 2).

"Think about it," he contin-ues. "We give dogs what time we can spare, what space we can spare, what food we can spare, and what love we can spare. In return, dogs give us their all. It's the best deal we human beings have ever made" (2009b, p. 2).

Dog parks provide an opportunity for users to enhance the special relationship they have with their dogs.

If you can be cheerful, ignor-ing aches and pains;

If you can resist complain-ing and boring people with your troubles;

If you can eat the same food every day and be grateful for it;

If you can understand when loved ones are too busy to give you any time;

If you can take criticism and blame without resentment;

If you can face the world without lies and deceit;

If you can start the day without caffeine or pep pills;

If you can relax without liquor and sleep without the aid of drugs;

If you can find great happiness in the simplest things in life;

If you can forgive any action in the blink of an eye;

If you can repel intruders without using lethal weapons;

If you have no bias against creed, color, religion, politics, or gender;

If you offer unconditional love as naturally as you breathe;

. . . then you are almost as good as your dog.

Richard Lederer

Dog parks are, after all, *parks*. They should be welcoming, attractive, desirable, and well-maintained community resources.

What Is a Dog Park?

To define just what a dog park is, you need a simple, straightforward description so everyone will have the same picture, more or less, in their mind's eye. That said, the following definition is simple, but accurate:

> A *dog park* is a space, often in a public park and usually enclosed with fencing, where dogs can run and play, off leash, with their owners and other dogs.

Let's look at this definition further by clarifying the various terms for our particular context.

In the previous definition, the "space" refers to property with the following qualities: usually mostly cleared; often with several trees; usually sunny but with some shade; level, sloped, or with a variety of grades; and, preferably, at least an acre in size. Ideally, the surface is grassy, but other types of surfacing are common and acceptable.

"Often in a public park" refers to the fact that, although some dog parks are standalone facilities, most are located within a public park or on public property. Dog parks may also be found on private properties and communities, and some are in commercial locations.

"Fencing" refers to the enclosure that establishes the dog park's perimeter. Chain-link fences are most common, but other types are acceptable. Considerations include recommended heights, installation needs, and several types of gates to choose from.

"Off leash" means that pets are unleashed within the confines of the dog park.

Throughout the book, several other terms are explained. Some will require more explanation than others, but none are too technical or cumbersome. Some aspects of dog parks have several terms with the same meaning. Some differ from one geographic region to another.

Perhaps the most important thing to remember is that dog parks are within the general category of park facilities. Thus, many accepted terms relating to park facilities apply. Terms such as *maintenance*, *landscaping*, *shade*, *screening*, *signage*, *grade*, *surface replenishment*, and *components* reflect specific needs and applications of dog parks.

The Need for Dog Parks

Clearly, the passion we have for our pets is reflected in the many statistics discussed here. Whether it's the sheer number of pets throughout the United States, the money we spend on our pets, or the wonderful health benefits exhibited by research, pets are a vital aspect of our society. They are an important part of our lives and families. They travel with us, they celebrate with us, they appear in our photographs, and on and on. For many, pets are about quality of life. Our lives are richer, more fulfilling, and, let's face it, more fun because of our pets. Is it any wonder that the popularity of dog parks has practically exploded throughout the United States? We humans have always enjoyed *our* parks, but it is wonderful for our dogs to have parks of their own, a place for them to run and play and socialize, just as we do. Plus, we get to watch them having fun—how terrific is that?

This book is all about making that happen. It takes that passion, that joy that dog owners feel and express, and turns it into the enthusiastic desire and drive to create a special park facility for both people and their beloved pets to experience and enjoy. In this book, you will learn all about how to create these very special places.

It's important to point out how developing community dog parks is in perfect alignment with the mission of most parks departments and agencies. These typically include statements about maintaining and enhancing quality of life, along with the importance of acquiring, developing, and preserving parks, recreation areas, open space, and facilities. Mission statements also often refer to meeting the needs of changing and growing communities by promoting and providing opportunities for residents and guests to enjoy meaningful, enjoyable leisure experiences through safe parks and recreation facilities. In addition, many park agencies' mission statements mention the importance of providing a variety of personal, social, and economic benefits for folks to play, relax, and meet others in natural environments. How wonderfully does all this apply to dog parks? Obviously, the contribution dog parks make to communities' well-being and quality of life, especially as reflected in these mission statements, couldn't be more fitting!

Now let's head into the early stages of a community contemplating a dog park—the typical ways that one is initiated and the various types of benefits that should be discussed and reviewed. Thus, with user-friendly information, let's begin the next chapter by barking up the right tree!

Making the Case

No matter how excited you are about a dog park, you can be sure that some people will not share the enthusiasm. With patience and positive education, you can address concerns and highlight the advantages of the planned park!

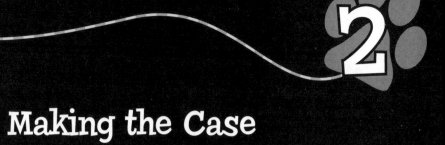

A community's interest in a dog park may be initiated in several ways. It often takes the action of just a few residents, usually dog owners or dog lovers, who may write a letter to a city council, stop by the local parks and recreation department to talk, or show up at a municipal meeting to express their interest in a public setting. These beginnings, or variations of these examples, are very common. Or, a dog park may be initiated by municipal employees, often parks and recreation administrators. Sometimes local politicians express interest in the community developing a dog park. I know of a county executive from a northeastern state who encountered dog parks for the first time while vacationing with his wife and their dog in Florida. Upon returning from his vacation, he immediately contacted the county parks administrator and requested that work begin on a dog park for the county. (This was to be a traditional fenced off-leash area, since recent signage to discourage owners from letting dogs run uncontrolled throughout the park hadn't worked. Their signs indicating that all dogs must be leashed simply prompted owners to attach leashes to their dogs' collars, but they weren't holding the other end of the leash! The leashes were just trailing along the ground behind the dogs!)

Addressing Naysayers

Regardless of how a community dog park is initiated, it may be met with resistance. This is often the case for locations where dog parks are considered a new concept, where many are unfamiliar with dog parks, or where residents feel it's an unneeded, unwise use of municipal funds. This is especially true if this is to be the *first* dog park in a particular area or city. Many cities, after experiencing the popularity of dog parks, create several parks in different neighborhoods, since residents may request the convenience of one closer to their home. In addition, a number of cities with numerous dog parks have established standards for creating them that make it far easier and more cost-efficient for future dog park development—thus, no need to reinvent the wheel. In these situations, of course, the growing pains typically reflecting resistance are often nonexistent.

The resistance, when it comes, may take many forms. It may be about anticipated noise or barking, problems concerning owners not picking up after their dogs, the expected foul smell, the municipal funding ("You're going to build a park for dogs when we need more soccer fields and playgrounds for children?"), health concerns, dog fights, and so on. Some will complain about the selected location ("I like the idea of a dog park, I just don't want it there!") or NIMBY issues (i.e., Not In My Back Yard). Most of these concerns relate to a lack of information or understanding, but those in opposition might simply dislike dogs. Some may have had a negative personal experience with a dog and have had a fear of them since that time. Others have visited poorly designed or poorly maintained dog parks and have come away with a negative impression. Still others have heard negative stories about dog parks. All these, and more, are verbalized concerns that you may encounter. However, you can address virtually all of them with solid, quality education. You can provide education about these concerns in several ways:

- Offer public informational presentations at your city hall, a community center, library, or at community organization meetings.
- Distribute informational publications at a variety of community locations or send them to households along with other municipal items, such as the parks and recreation program brochures.
- Advertise through local television or radio presentations.
- Provide information through the Internet, perhaps on the community's website.

These examples of ways you can disseminate information about dog parks should certainly help change minds, at least for open-minded residents. Be aware, however, as with so many community issues, that some people will be unmoved, despite your best efforts. The idea of a dog park, to them, may remain controversial. In most cases, however, if you present the material well, people will begin to get excited about the prospect of a dog park in *their* city!

So let's look at some of those concerns, one by one, and consider how they can be addressed. I'll expand on some of these points made by naysayers later on.

The first hurdle here is the simplest: just the *idea* of a dog park may be upsetting to some who are unfamiliar with this type of facility! "Who ever heard of such a thing? Ridiculous!" Quite honestly, *my* initial reaction years ago was similar. However, I quickly then thought, "Really? Can it be what it sounds like? A park for dogs? How cool!" Then I simply had to learn more! Many folks, though, aren't so quick to respond positively. Without any knowledge or experience, it's hard to blame them for being critical and finding the concept absurd. Thus, the need for education and understanding, as mentioned previously, is clear.

Safety

One of the most common concerns, especially for those unfamiliar with dog parks, relates to worries about dog fights. Fights between dogs can and do happen. However, perhaps surprisingly, they are rare! The majority of fights between dogs concern territorial issues. In a dog park, there are so many different smells and scents that it's a no-man's-land, or rather, a no-dog's-land, when it comes to whose territory is whose. Thus, without territory concerns, dogs freely socialize, play, run, and generally have fun with one another. Those unfamiliar with the concept of dog parks usually find this downright amazing and hard to believe. The reality, of course, is that if this were not the case, there would be no dog parks!

Two uncommon issues that may contribute to fights, though quite infrequent, relate to stress and guarding of resources. What looks like stress in a dog can simply be excitement—they are often thrilled to come to the dog park! Owners should *know* their dogs; they need to recognize their dog's behaviors and be able to identify when a problem might occur. When dogs first arrive at the park for a visit, other dogs already inside may run to greet the new visitor at the entrance. This is extremely common. For the most part, it's not only usually harmless, it can appear downright endearing—a veritable doggy welcome wagon! However, a good-sized gang of dogs meeting and greeting can make the newcomer feel threatened or vulnerable. When owners know their dog as they

Most dogs in the park will rush to greet new arrivals.

should, they can learn ways to handle this situation to avoid a problem. Again, most dogs deal with this just fine, but owners must take responsibility for learning their dog's park behaviors. Resource guarding is really about owners bringing their dog's toys or similar items into a dog park. Again, this may be an infrequent problem, but owners must heed the park rules, which often indicate these items should not be brought into the dog park. So again, owners must be vigilant about knowing their dog's behavior and complying with a dog park's rules. As stated previously, if these types of issues were a common concern in dog parks, there probably wouldn't be dog parks!

Legal Concerns

Some folks raise the issue of liability. They may be concerned about a municipality's insurance. Frequently, this question is raised by the municipality's governing board, often in a public setting. This is an understandable concern. To respond, I often quote from the website www.dogbitelaw.com, under suits against local governments:

> The victim of a personal injury or injury to the victim's dog probably will not prevail on a claim against the local government entity that established the dog park. Generally, there are immunities that protect government entities from many claims; if the entity believed that it was doing something beneficial for the community, it is hard to get around the immunity.

In addition, under assumption of the risk,

> If you go to a no-leash dog park and you are injured by a dog, under circumstances other than a bite where the dog would not have injured you if it was leashed, then there is a very good argument that you assumed the risk. After all, you knew that leashes were optional at the park, but you went there anyway to take advantage of the same leash-optional law that resulted in your own injuries.

Thus, municipalities are protected when they create a dog park, much as they are covered though municipal insurance for other park facilities. It is important to point out, however, that municipalities must build and operate their facilities according to specific safety standards, some of which may be regulated by law. This is covered in more detail in chapter 4.

Cleanliness

Next is a concern about owners picking up after their dogs. This is very possibly the single most important issue in successful dog parks. Simply, dog parks work because users *must* pick up their dogs' feces. This self-enforcement aspect of dog parks is universal. Most users do indeed take this rule very seriously. Thus, the importance of owners observing and monitoring their dogs is obvious. Owners typically nudge each another when one hasn't noticed that their dog just went and, just as typically, no offense is taken. Often, you may even hear a "thank you" as the owner goes over to retrieve and dispose of their dog's feces. I am forever telling communities that the maintenance of a dog park does *not* involve park staff picking up feces! This is exclusively the responsibility of the users. I also often explain that if this wasn't an accepted standard, a mandatory rule that must be obeyed by all users, dog parks wouldn't work, they wouldn't be the wildly popular park facilities they've become, and, more likely, they wouldn't exist. Thus, the naysayers must understand that users will be required to pick up after their dogs at all times. Those who don't follow the dog park rules, as with

It's in everyone's best interest to keep the dog park clean, and they generally do.

other park facility usage, will not be permitted to use the community dog park. I have often heard that since an owner may occasionally, inadvertently, miss their dog defecating, owners frequently pick up nearby excrement from other dogs when picking up after their own. They reason that they'd hope someone would do that for them if they miss picking up once in a while. It's certainly in everyone's best interests to keep the community dog park clean, well maintained, and feces free. Again, this rule is a serious, absolute necessity to maintaining a successful, quality dog park facility.

Noise and Air Pollution

The barking or noise issue is quite common. The fact is that most dog parks are not particularly noisy. Dogs are usually content: having fun, enjoying the socializing, and playing with other dogs or people. Some say there's really nothing to bark about. That tends to be the case. However, it may just take one barker to get the whole gang going! Thus, I always suggest that a community include, as one of their dog park rules, "Nuisance or excessive barking should be discouraged." Depending on the dog park's proximity to residential areas, this would be particularly important in the early morning and evening. Since self-enforcement is key in *all* dog parks, all users must take this rule seriously. Sometimes, if felt necessary, the rule can be made more stringent by adding a phrase indicating that owners should remove their dog from the park if the barking cannot be controlled. That said, suggested dog park etiquette (see chapter 6) indicates that a problem barker may be an inappropriate candidate for dog park usage. Again, however, in the majority of dog parks, noisy barking is *not* a problem.

The concern about smell obviously relates directly to the previous one about owners picking up after their dogs. Thus, this is another important reason for that rule. I seldom encounter a dog park that smells unpleasant. Urine usually dissipates, and periodic rain helps that process, further deterring odor. When users regularly pick up after their dogs and use securely covered trash receptacles which I always recommend, an offensive smell is simply not a problem in dog parks. The one exception I must mention, however, concerns wood-chip surfacing, which I always discourage. Among a number of problems with this type of surfacing, wood chips absorb urine, which may cause an odor. This should not occur with other types of surfacing. Again, though, dog parks generally do not smell bad.

Funding

The municipal funding issue—especially the idea of spending tax dollars on dogs rather than, say, on children—can often cause great controversy. I always point out, perhaps tongue in cheek, that dog parks are *not* for dogs, they are for their owners. I quickly add that dogs don't vote. I then discuss other park facilities selected and used for particular constituencies: ball fields for Little Leaguers and adult softball players, tennis courts for tennis players, swimming pools for swimmers, and so on. The fact is, I continue to explain, that there are probably more dog owners in a community than all those other various constituencies put together! In addition, developing a dog park may very well cost less, often substantially less, than many, if not most, other park facilities.

Also in regard to the concerns about costs, some communities may tell those residents interested in a dog park that there simply is no money to build one. Especially during difficult economic times, municipalities are often uninterested in capital projects in general, let alone a new park facility, with controversy no less! They may say, however, that if the interested parties are willing to fundraise, the powers that be might consider such a proposal. Frankly, this scenario is quite common. The municipality then often provides the space, either in an existing park or on available municipal property, and the interested residents form a nonprofit organization to raise funds to build the dog park. In addition to the fundraising, the group often has needed items donated, such as fencing, site work, and benches. Two extremely important cautionary notes here: (1) Items donated to the dog park, such as benches, must be of heavy-duty commercial grade, *not* for residential use, and (2) most importantly, the municipality must be willing to oversee the project and take full responsibility for the operation of the completed dog park (usually through the parks and recreation department). Chapter 4 explains more about these responsibilities.

Finally, I must comment on the unfortunate practice of charging fees for dog park usage. I strongly believe that, like picnic tables, open fields, and playgrounds in public parks, dog parks should be available free of charge and never recommend charging fees of any type. Often when there is a negative reaction to a suggested dog park, the response is to charge a small, affordable fee. However, this topic needs serious consideration if a community deems it necessary because there are many consequences of charging a fee for dog park usage such as the following:

- Fees may limit the number of dogs encountered when visiting the dog park. Dog parks are usually about the idea of "the more, the merrier" and the experience is not nearly as much fun when there are fewer dogs.

- Fees, often coupled with residency restrictions, keep owners from bringing friends and relatives to the park to show off their off-leash facility and encouraging them to create dog parks in their communities.

- When fees are charged, there are costs to the municipality that may offset the revenue to a certain extent (e.g., administrative costs, record-keeping costs, enforcement costs).

- Fees and restrictions may minimize the economic benefits of a dog park by discouraging visitors to the dog park who would be likely to spend money in the community.

These concerns from naysayers are among the most common ones. In a given community, site-specific concerns may come up that must be addressed. These often relate to residences adjacent to the proposed site, even if the dog park is planned in an existing park. Again, especially if this will be a new facility in a region where many folks are not yet familiar with dog parks, you can expect many questions at best, and downright anger at worst. Those who have a fear of dogs, or whose children are afraid of dogs, for example, may be quite vocal. Those types of naysayers' fears should be handled in a sensitive, understanding manner. Assure them that they will never need to be worried about dogs running loose in an existing park outside the perimeter of the new dog park.

Actually, one of the benefits of a creating a dog park in an existing park facility is that it becomes easier to prohibit dogs off leash throughout the rest of the park. In communities where off-leash dogs have been an ongoing problem, this is a particularly helpful advantage of dog parks.

Again, the key to responding to the naysayers and their concerns is, not surprisingly, education. These folks, one way or another, must have their concerns addressed. You can do this in a number of ways, but you must convey correct, appropriate information. Knowledgeable park professionals should be able to respond intelligently and supportively, as with any controversial situation. Of course, it's always important to remember that some folks will remain unconvinced. Those with an open mind who are receptive to learning about dog parks will usually not be disappointed. You can distribute the information in written form, using newspaper articles, brochures, handout sheets in schools, libraries, shops, and so on. Verbal form, such as through radio or television interviews or by using speakers at community organization meetings or community informational presentations, like public hearings, can also be effective. You can certainly use the Internet to help educate the community. It's a matter of getting the word out with factual, understandable information to answer questions and allay fears.

Benefits of a Dog Park

The benefits provided by a community dog park are many. People are often surprised by these because some of the advantages are seldom thought of as important. Some benefits are simple pluses that are often taken for granted. For example, a dog park is often made by simply adding a venue to an existing park. It may be yet another reason a park is popular, enjoyed by many throughout the community. A mayor from a small Connecticut town once indicated that an unexpected bonus of their new dog park was that it attracted very different members of the community, thus helping residents communicate and become friends who probably would have never even met otherwise! Talk about community cohesiveness! Many would never realize these very simple, but understandable, important benefits of a dog park.

- **Dog parks give pets the opportunity to exercise and socialize in a safe environment.** Most dogs want and need exercise. They are also very social animals, and most greatly enjoy playing with other dogs. An inherent part of being a dog owner is the responsibility of walking your pet—to give dogs the opportunity both to exercise and to defecate outside. Some dog owners may have physical difficulty walking their dog or time constraints, or they may simply feel they'd like their pet to play with other dogs. A dog park can provide an alternative to regular dog walking. Plus, the dog park experience can offer dogs so much more than a simple walk. They can safely run, play, and have fun with other dogs under the watchful eyes of their owners.

Another important point is that, in a dog park, pets are far less likely to encounter cars, bicycles, people on inline skates or skateboards, and so on. Thus, dog parks truly provide a safer environment.

Active, safe play provides great exercise, fun, and socialization opportunities.

- **Dog parks promote responsible pet ownership.** Dog owners should realize the importance of their pet's needs for exercise, play, exploration, and, ideally, socialization. Dog parks provide these opportunities and more. These activities should take place under the watchful eye of owners. In addition, they should take place in a safe, appropriate location where owners follow needed rules, such as picking up after their dogs. All of these aspects of responsible pet ownership are available, and they can be easily and safely provided in a dog park. The presence of a dog park facility in a community also encourages dog owners to use an appropriate location for these activities rather than an open, unfenced area in a park (or other location), where they may not feel the need to pick up after their dog or follow other rules typical in dog parks. (When communities develop an off-leash facility, they often then no longer allow dogs in other public parks.)

- **Dog parks provide apartment dwellers, elderly people, and disabled pet owners with an accessible place to exercise their dogs.** "If it wasn't for our dog park, I couldn't have a dog." Some dog owners don't have a backyard or an appropriate area nearby to walk their dogs. Some are themselves unable to walk, or have difficulty walking by themselves, let alone with a dog! Dog parks thus provide an important necessity for these people who want to enjoy dog ownership. It is also important to remember that dog parks in the United States, as are all public parks, must be accessible to all in compliance with the Americans with Disabilities Act.

- **Dog parks promote enforcement of dog control laws.** Typically, dog control laws refer to important general rules related to dog ownership, often about licensing and vaccinations. These types of laws are usually also reflected in a dog park's rules and regulations. For dog owners to use their local dog park, they must comply with the facility's requirements. Thus, they comply with dog control laws that they might otherwise ignore. In addition, it is far easier for a municipality's animal control officer to check required licenses and tags (proof of vaccinations) in a dog park than in perhaps any other community location.

Another important aspect of this benefit is that dog parks, as specific areas designed for off-leash activities, lessen the likelihood that owners will unleash their dogs in other parks where pets are either allowed only on a leash or not at all. Also, as mentioned earlier, many communities that create a dog park no longer allow dogs in their other public parks.

- **Dog parks are added attractions for parks that cater to a specific, large, legitimate constituency.** Just as a community has its soccer players, swimmers, softball and baseball players, tennis and basketball enthusiasts, and so on, dog owners represent an important portion of the population who also want to use a particular park feature. Plus, in most communities, dog owners may very well represent a larger group than all the soccer players, swimmers, softball and baseball players, and tennis and basketball enthusiasts put together! They indeed represent an important large constituency that should be viewed as just as deserving of a particular facility as others who require specialized venues, such as sports fields, tennis courts, and swimming pools.

- **Dog parks provide a municipality with an additional park venue not unlike ball fields, tennis and basketball courts, and swimming pools.** Similar to the previous benefit, it is a simple fact that dog parks add to community resources. In many cases, a dog park may be one of the least expensive park facilities to create, yet it often provides the biggest bang for the buck.

- **Dog parks provide an opportunity for dog owners to meet and socialize.** In some communities, this aspect of a local dog park is an extremely popular one! Friendships are made and fostered while the dogs have fun. Users, of course, encounter other dog owners and, often, dog *lovers*. Having these interests in common can make for wonderful relationships for both people and dogs. Often, dog owners come to a dog park from many different localities within a municipality. They may be not only from different neighborhoods but also from different cultures, backgrounds, or even economic circumstances. They may very well never have otherwise met one another, and yet, in a dog park, they share the commonality of dog ownership. The social benefits of a dog park are particularly good for singles and folks who live alone. Where other park facilities focus on providing for particular ages, abilities, or interests, a dog park can reach nearly everyone in a community.

- **Dog owners love to watch their dogs at play (though many people, including those without dogs, enjoy watching pets play in a dog park).** This is a particularly enjoyable benefit of a local dog park. It's simply fun to watch dogs play with one another. For dog owners, it's important to always watch and monitor your dog's behavior, but it's enjoyable to do so as well. For those who are not dog owners, it's still another park venue they can enjoy as a spectator. However, unlike a sports activity, there are no winners or losers. Dog parks thus provide a place anyone can enjoy, and most tend to be smiling as they watch!

It's not just dogs who socialize in a dog park!

- **Dog parks promote public health and safety.** Well-exercised dogs are better neighbors who are less likely to create a nuisance, bark excessively, or destroy property. In many cases, it may simply be because all the playing, running, and socializing tires a dog out. In addition, dogs may realize that the dog park is *their* place to play. With the owners monitoring as required, the dogs often learn appropriate behaviors in the dog park setting. This helps *everyone* in a community!

- **Dog parks have genuine multigenerational characteristics.** Though most dog parks have some rules concerning young children, everyone can happily use a dog park together, including older children, teens, and adults at any age. Since a variety of family members can enjoy a park facility at the same time with their pets, the multigenerational bonding opportunities are obvious.

- **Dog parks have reportedly caused decreases in antisocial and illegal activities in public parks.** Troublemakers are less likely to use a public park with an active off-leash facility. Drug use, for example, has decreased in parks where dog park facilities have been developed.

- **Dog parks offer economic benefits for their communities.** Visitors to dog parks often spend money in a variety of community venues. They may stop to pick up a pizza, purchase an item in a local pharmacy, or even just buy a newspaper. Those are all dollars spent because of the dog park! Or, better yet, perhaps a visitor notes a particular store or business he or she wants to return to with friends or family—a furniture store, a car dealership, or a new restaurant. Those dollars all add up!

- **Constituents appreciate their dog parks!** Perhaps more so than about almost any other park feature, users often happily tell others how much they enjoy and appreciate their local dog parks. In fairness, dog parks may still be a bit of a novelty in many areas. Thus, they get more attention than, say, a new soccer field, but it must be remembered that they provide a resource for a far greater percentage of the population than a new soccer field does. In addition, brand-new users are often amazed at these facilities. They don't hesitate to tell friends, neighbors, and, often, local politicians how much they *love* their local dog park! Politicians who supported the creation of a community dog park but may have been hesitant to the new concept are often amazed as well. "We should have created this years ago!"

One last note here, not really a benefit of dog parks but an important point nonetheless, is that unlike people who get bored visiting their local park repeatedly, perhaps wishing for improvements or new features, dogs *never* tire of their dog park. Instead they look forward to their visits more and more where there are new and familiar dog pals, new smells, new people, and so on.

Next, let's review the various considerations that must be taken into account when exploring a dog park project. Though the concept is not a difficult one, you must certainly consider a number of important aspects, including location, parking, and accessibility, to name but a few. The next chapter reflects on these concerns and others to maximize the opportunity to create a quality, top-notch off-leash facility.

As we begin to look at these considerations, I can't help but feel a bit jealous. To create a wonderful dog park facility, no dogs need to think about getting a mortgage, a down payment, points, closing costs, inspections, home repairs, or maintenance. Is that fair?

Planning

Let's get the dog park started! You'll need to garner support, select a site, and much more.

What to do? How to do it? After all, we've never built one of these facilities—ball fields, swimming pools, and tennis courts, yes; dog parks, no!

If you are charged with determining the feasibility and potential value of creating an off-leash facility for your community, what should you consider? What are the important items you need to think about, look for, and decide on when determining whether to initiate a dog park project? Where do we begin? What are potential problems? In addition, what must you avoid, and how do you move forward to minimize issues and maximize the potential success of the facility?

This chapter addresses these concerns and considerations. Park professionals should endeavor to comprehensively learn, acknowledge, and evaluate the available information about dog parks, and then focus on their community's specific needs and desires. In addition, resources and support must, of course, be considered important aspects of this exercise. Resources should include property or land for the new facility, as well as potential funding sources. Although support often reflects a financial component, it can also refer to the attitudes of local politicians and municipal staff, as well as community members' interests, or lack thereof, in developing a dog park. That important topic, support, is where we begin our discussion of dog park considerations.

Community and Political Support

The fact that the idea of creating a dog park has, one way or another, become a topic of conversation or interest in a community usually means that some information must be gathered. Who are the most interested community members? Have they made themselves known? Are they actively advocating for the municipality to create an off-leash facility? If needed, are they willing to and interested in helping raise funds for the project? On the other hand, does the community need to raise funds, or can the needed funds perhaps be budgeted? Or might the necessary funding for the new dog park be obtained other ways? What about the attitudes of the municipality's political leaders? Are they positive or negative? Do leaders need to be educated about dog parks?

With these very realistic examples in mind, it's always beneficial to get your ducks in a row before tackling what might be a controversial endeavor. Obviously, you want a positive, enthusiastic start to the project, so some preliminary behind-the-scenes work may be very helpful. This can involve some research, discussions with knowledgeable people who are familiar with dog parks, or conversations with park professionals who have already created, and now administer and maintain, off-leash facilities.

Educating various factions of a community to develop and encourage support may be a helpful strategy. Information provided could involve written materials, such as brochures, fliers, or articles in community newsletters, local newspapers, or in seasonal literature from the parks and recreation program. In addition, you could distribute information through the Internet, local radio or television, or in a community meeting setting.

Dog park supporters who have artistic talent or perhaps experience in graphic design can help the cause in numerous ways. A logo or graphics for the proposed

A creative, attractive logo brings identity to a community dog park.

dog park can identify and promote the project to the public on fliers, brochures, and other types of published information about the dog park. Publicity and signage using visual recognition is always a plus for support.

Support from community residents and local politicians can often make or break a dog park project. Park professionals must realize the importance of this and must do what they can to develop, nurture, and maintain this support. Even when that support seems to come naturally, with sincere encouragement, this positive, helpful interest should not be taken for granted.

Naming the Dog Park

Though this is a very early stage in a dog park project, it may be the best time to name the park! A name coupled with a new logo can help rally support, provide recognition for the proposed facility, and can certainly assist with publicity and, eventually, marketing. It can be as simple as the name of the community followed by *dog park* or it can creatively reflect a particular aspect of the city or town, perhaps something historical or related to a municipality's nickname or some other aspect of significance to a community. You could even hold a contest to name the dog park to garner attention and help publicize a sense of excitement, fun, and interest about the proposed project.

One note of caution, however: Naming a dog park a Bark Park, though popular, is *not* a good idea. It sends the wrong message, especially to the anti–dog park folks, who may interpret that name to mean a park with a hoard of barking dogs—a noisy and perhaps unruly vision, indeed! In all the development stages, supporters need to do everything they can to communicate the dog park information in a positive light. The name selected for the dog park should promote and emphasize the sense of community value, not detract from it. Thus, the name of the dog park is actually an important, helpful step in the development process signifying that a new, exciting park facility is truly on its way!

Financial Support

A dog park can be relatively inexpensive to build, compared with other park facilities, depending on how many amenities are planned. Each park is different, and a wide range of possible features may be planned, depending on the community's needs and resources. Some features are mandatory:

- **Fencing and gates**. These will be the most costly items by far.
- **Benches**. Plan to place several in each enclosed area.
- **Waste-bag stations**. The park must have at least one near the entry and at least one in each enclosed area.
- **Covered waste cans**. The park must have at least one near the entry and at least one in each enclosed area.
- **Water fountains for dogs and people**. Ideally, the park should have one fountain in each enclosed area; if only one fountain is available for the whole park, it should be placed in the transition entry space.
- **Shade structures** (as needed). If these will provide the only shade in the park, several will be needed in each area, some for dogs, some for dog owners.
- **Hardscape**. Hardscape refers to hard, non-grass surfaces such as pavement and is needed at least for the transition area and entry aprons for each of the enclosed areas; ideally, it will also be present under benches and the other items to facilitate easier maintenance.
- **Signage**. You will need at least two signs: one welcome or entry sign with the dog park name and one with the rules and emergency information.

Other features are optional. They are nice to have, but are not required, and they may possibly even be problematic in some cases:

- **Landscaping or flowers**. This can be minimal. Landscape *outside* of the dog park enclosures, next to the welcome or entry sign with the dog park's name.
- **Fire hydrant**. This dog park fixture is traditional and fun, and can be brightly painted.
- **Play equipment**. I recommend buying this *only* from safe commercial manufacturers who specialize in dog park equipment.
- **Sculpture**. Permanent installations should be substantially heavy duty and weatherproof.
- **Agility equipment**. This should be of substantial, professional, commercial quality (i.e., not homemade), but it can be portable (used when needed and stored when not in use).

- **Aquatic facility**. This choice can be expensive and may need to meet local health department regulations. (Sometimes a natural body of water is nearby and may be accessible, but it should not be a part of the dog park.)

All of these features are discussed in greater detail in chapter 4. They are listed here to offer a starting point for estimating potential costs of building a dog park.

Funding is always a huge concern, as with any park development project. The cost factor, similar to the factor of community and political support, will have an enormous effect on how and when, or even *if*, you will open your dog park.

Of course, funding is necessary, but an off-leash facility often easily attracts donors and offers a greater variety of ways to contribute than many other park development endeavors do. In addition, many communities can offer in-kind assistance, especially municipalities with various department employees who can install fencing, benches, and water lines, or pour footings and install hardscape surfaces. These labor-oriented tasks, when done commercially, often greatly increase the amount of funding needed. Otherwise, items such as benches, water fountains, shade structures, and other dog park components are often happily donated, especially when an individual, company, or organization name can be permanently linked to the item with a plaque or another type of signage. Often, a community offers a wish list of items to residents with the needed dollar amounts indicated to donate the cost. Do not request various items be donated directly. (Most of the needed items are commercial ones intended for public park usage, and they are often selected to match existing items in park facilities. These typically include benches, signage, water fountains, and waste

Personalized fundraising bricks are a popular way to both fund the dog park and create a needed, attractive hardscape for the facility.

containers.) Instead, ask that contributors donate according to a predetermined cost for specific selected items.

Perhaps one of the most popular donation programs for dog parks is the use of fundraising bricks. These bricks can be attractively used for some or all of the various hard surfaces throughout the dog park: in the entry areas, under the water fountains or benches, and so on. They are typically purchased for a specific amount and engraved with the donor's name or with a message from the donor honoring or memorializing someone, frequently a pet. The donation amount is several times the actual cost of the brick and engraving, thus, allowing people to contribute to the project and be recognized at a reasonable cost.

It is not unusual to receive larger contributions for the creation of a dog park. These usually depend on specific resources available in a particular community. For example, a fencing contractor who is a dog lover may contribute a portion of the fencing materials, a local sign company may contribute the needed signage, or an excavator may contribute by conducting site work or grading. Often, the savings related to these types of contributions can be enormous!

Sometimes, grants may be available for constructing a dog park. Obtaining a grant, of any amount, usually involves people who are knowledgeable and experienced with grants, grant writing, and related research. Government staff members or savvy residents may use grant-related skills and creativity to apply for (and hopefully obtain) grant monies to develop a dog park.

There are currently several companies offering contests and programs to assist with dog park costs. For example, Beneful offers a Dream Dog Park makeover contest, PetSafe has a Bark for Your Park program, and the Room to Run Dog Park Appreciation Project is sponsored by Nutro.

Finally, a community may decide to simply budget the costs to build a dog park. This may be more common when the community already has a dog park and determines that they need another one or more, often in a different neighborhood or area of the municipality. They realize that a dog park is one of the least expensive park venues to develop, yet it is one of the most regularly used and appreciated. Whether the dog park development is placed in a queue as a capital project or in an annual municipal budget, some communities may simply treat it as a desirable, needed park improvement.

Site Selection

Selecting an appropriate site for a community off-leash area is often one of the earliest concerns discussed when the idea of creating a dog park first surfaces. Initially, suggestions may be plentiful, as they should be, but realistic options become apparent when priorities are determined and evaluated.

In most cases, the site selected will be either in an existing park or on property owned by the community that is underused or not used at all. The property may not even be maintained. Of particular importance is the size of the available land. Ideally, an acre is considered the standard minimum. Smaller spaces can be used, but they will often generate problems not present in larger off-leash areas. Bigger is generally better. In some regions, dog parks are considerably larger than an acre; often, multiple acres are preferred. In areas such as the Northeast United States, however, available land is extremely limited; thus, finding an appropriate site can be quite challenging.

Most of the remaining considerations reviewed in this chapter relate, at least to some extent, to this topic of site selection.

Topography and Sight Lines

The site need not be level, but all areas should offer clear sight lines. In other words, the entire space to be used for the park should easily enable users to monitor their dogs; there should be no areas where dogs will be hidden from view. That's not to say the site must be totally clear; it should simply not have peaks and valleys that prevent owners from seeing their pets. Fencing placement may either cause these types of site problems or alleviate them. The same is true in relation to bench placement.

It's also important to point out that a level, open space is, in several respects, *not* desirable, but it may be improved. Though thickly wooded areas would indeed be problematic for monitoring dogs, lightly wooded areas or groups of trees spread out over an area add interest, attractiveness, and needed shade to a dog park. Even a large rock or boulder here and there can provide interest or natural focal points. However, care should be taken in the area designated for

Natural elements offer many advantages in a dog park. Wooded areas and trees provide beauty and shade, while rock outcroppings add interest to the visual landscape.

small dogs regarding the size of trees or other items, since it may be more difficult to see smaller dogs in and around these features. Remember, too, that features can be added to the site—shade structures, commercial or local sculpture, trees, and so on—to provide interest and attractiveness. Some communities may even highlight donated features. As always, these types of items must be appropriate for an outdoor, public park application; they must be sturdy, weather resistant, safe, and easy to maintain.

Access to Water

Ideally, the proximity to water access should be a major consideration in the site selection. A dog fountain is a must for a dog park; thus, access to water is a must. Hopefully, especially if the designated site is in an existing park facility, a nearby water source is already available. Thus, it should be easy to extend it to the site to

A water fountain for dogs and people is a must in a dog park.

connect it to a new water fountain (or to several fountains). If the dog park is being built outside of an existing park, connecting to a municipal water line may be necessary. Drilling a well can be an expensive endeavor, so other ways to provide water may need to be explored. Since building a dog park without a fountain is problematic in several respects, the topic is discussed in the next chapter about components. Dog fountains are basically people fountains on the ground and are produced by several commercial manufacturers. The fountains are all basically the same—they come in a variety of colors (and graffiti-resistant textures) and with a number of great options, several of which I always recommend. Options include things like people fountains attached atop the dog fountains, fountains at a level accessible to kids and people with disabilities, bibs for hose attachments, and attached hand-wash stations. No guidelines exist on the particular number of fountains a dog park (or any park for that matter) should have. This lack of guidelines also applies to the other items, such as the number of waste cans, benches, and shade structures. The usage may cause communities to add benches, waste-bag stations, or more signage. (I consider the need for more of these types of items a good thing—people are using and enjoying the dog park, perhaps more so than had been expected!)

Proximity to Other Park Venues

When selecting a site for a dog park in an existing park, though it may seem desirable to have other park features nearby, it is not recommended, since problems can result from this proximity. For example, a nearby ball field, tennis court, or playground, which are standard park components, may inadvertently encourage dog owners to leave their dogs in the off-leash enclosure while they watch a ball game, play a round of tennis, or supervise their children on the playground—all of which are realistic potential distractions that can easily keep owners from monitoring their dogs in the dog park. These, and all possible nearby distractions, should be avoided when evaluating sites for a new dog park. The site must be such that it encourages monitoring and supervision of the dogs. Although the posted rules and related signage will make it clear that dogs should never be unattended (and thus, unmonitored) in the facility, the location's proximity to other park features can make that rule difficult or easy to facilitate. If the location selection is limited and it is necessary to place the dog park site closer than advised to another park feature, in most cases, some type of screening can be created to provide at least a visual separation. Though not an optimum situation, screening can be an acceptable alternative, especially when combined with specific, additional subjective signage to alert users to the importance of constantly monitoring their dogs (despite the temptation to watch the big game at the football field adjacent to the dog park).

It should be noted, however, that in the case of a children's playground in the nearby vicinity of a proposed dog park site, screening and similar solutions may simply not be adequate. Parents, understandably, may decide to bring both a child and the family dog to the park. (After all, the playground and the dog park are next to one another.) This is a problem for the following reasons.

- Parents cannot monitor both their child and their dog at the same time— they must make a choice.

- Generally, children ought not to be in dog parks—often, communities establish age minimums, especially to discourage young children from being brought into the facility.

- Often, when a community develops a dog park, they create ordinances to disallow dogs in other park venues, even on leash. Thus, the parent should not take the dog to the playground or take (in many, if not most, cases) the child into the dog park.

- Obviously, the temptation is thus great for the parent to leave the dog unattended in the dog park and take the child to the playground—this is particularly likely if the two facilities are within easy view of each other. Thus, it's recommended that the dog park site selection not be located near a playground.

An exception to avoiding proximity to existing parks when selecting a dog park site is when there is a trail system that allows leashed dogs. Locating a dog park along an existing trail system encourages dog owners to walk to the dog park.

Plan your park so that people who use wheelchairs, walkers, and other orthopedic devices can access it with ease.

Accessibility

The Americans with Disabilities Act requires that a dog park be accessible to people with disabilities (who might be using a wheelchair or walker, for example). Park and recreation professionals usually know the importance of this, and need to plan accordingly. Thus, access must allow users with disabilities to enter the dog park area itself and also to get to the dog park from the street, the parking area, and so on. Usually, these considerations involve accessible surfacing, level ground, or an appropriate ramp system and gates of an appropriate minimum width. Since pet owners with disabilities primarily need to be able to enter the facility, not to maneuver through the entire area to use it, the larger issue may be getting to the dog park from the street or parking area, particularly if a slope or steps are involved. In many cases, this tends to be more of a problem than the direct entry into the dog park. It is recommended that a local, regional, or state ADA compliance officer be consulted if it appears that the lay of the land may be problematic in relation to accessibility. Typically, these professionals offer assistance and creative solutions, especially since the concern with accessibility compliance reflects a positive, caring attitude for a community's residents with disabilities. It is also, of course, simply the right thing to do.

Neighbors, Noise, and Odor

Considering community members residing in the area of a proposed dog park may or may not be tricky. It just takes one NIMBY (not in my backyard) neighbor to put a dog park project on hold indefinitely. Or, it may even be enough of a problem that an otherwise potentially good site may need to be eliminated. That may sometimes require seeking a new site and starting from scratch.

Obviously, when searching for a potential site to locate a new dog park, the proximity of neighbors must be taken into consideration. Typically, in most cases, that is why developing a dog park in an existing park facility may be preferred. Nearby neighbors are already used to the sights and sounds of frequent park activities—sports, events, various programs, lots of children, picnicking, and so on. However, even in this case, it's good to be proactive by telling residents early in the process that a dog park project is being considered in their neighborhood. Often, many neighbors may just ask for additional information. Some will be delighted, and others may be upset. As always, providing education and information may help. For example, as indicated in the previous chapter, dog parks are generally not noisy—though some dogs may bark a bit, most don't bark, and one of the more common park rules reminds dog owners to discourage their dogs from barking. Seldom is the noise of a dog park a problem for neighbors. Certainly, compared to a ball game or other frequent park activity, a dog park's noise is quite insignificant.

Possible odor from a dog park is an additional concern from neighbors that may need to be addressed. Also mentioned in the previous chapter, there is seldom a problem with odor in a dog park. As long as the posted rules emphasize the importance of picking up after your dog, having the needed waste bags, and securely closing waste containers conveniently available, most users will follow through and will often even remind others. Trash pickup, regardless of whose responsibility this will be, must be done regularly. These rules and tasks are all extremely important in a well-run, quality dog park. Between the responsibilities of the users and the sponsoring agency or owner of the dog park, these things must be done properly, or the dog park can and will be problematic. Moreover, if these types of problems were indeed common, successful dog parks would be few and far between. Of course, this is not the case. In other words, these concerns are typically not problems. Community members want their dog parks to be appropriately and happily used, with rules followed for everyone's enjoyment, benefit, and safety. Dog parks quickly become appreciated havens where most folks do what they can to make sure everyone respects the facility's rules. This is why most dog parks operate successfully. Otherwise, again, it is unlikely dog parks would even exist.

Parking

This actually may or may not be a realistic concern. It depends on the nature and type of community. Often, for example, the more urban an area is, the less likely the need for parking. Or, on the other hand, the more suburban a community is, the more parking will be needed. Offering nearby, convenient parking, as with any park facility, has become an important consideration in planning a new park venue. The parking area need not be paved, but it should be of adequate size, properly maintained, and, ideally, in close proximity to the transition area at the dog park's entry. If the dog park area is in an existing park, it is also desirable, if possible, that the users not have to walk past other park venues in the vicinity to get to the dog park entrance. This can be distracting and troublesome from several perspectives—even though the dogs are on leash being walked to the dog park entrance, they may pass a basketball court, playground, or ball field when play is in progress. The dogs may bark or want to join the exciting sights and sounds of the activities in progress, especially when children are the primary participants. Plus, the children may even call out to the dogs as they pass by. If possible, these opportunities for problematic behavior, on the part of dogs or the other park users, should be avoided when planning needed dog park parking.

Supervision

This consideration primarily refers to the ease of periodic supervision of the dog park by agency staff and police or animal control officers assigned to occasionally monitor the dog park. Their presence, though perhaps somewhat infrequent, offers opportunities to have positive interactions, to ask and answer questions, as well as to observe user behavior, especially compliance with the rules. In addition, the presence of these officials also helps maintain the feeling of a safe atmosphere in the park, which, at least in some dog parks, may be considered

Dogs can't wait to get into the dog park! Their owners will appreciate nearby parking that lets the dogs get right into the action.

very important to the users. Thus, the lay of the land for the parking area and driveway, or simply the street location of the park, should make it easy for any supervisory person to drive up to the facility's entry or fencing, exit (and reenter) their vehicle, and access the dog park enclosure to directly observe the usage and behavior of the dogs, the owners, and any other folks using the facility (or, for that matter, areas adjacent to the dog park, especially when safety is a concern). Even if supervisors are inclined to simply do an occasional drive-by, the dog park location and design should provide the ability to do this easily and well.

Maintenance

This consideration involves participation by the parks, grounds, or maintenance employees, ideally from the very beginning of interest in a dog park project. This is usually about turf and surfacing management (often simply mowing), waste removal, and refilling waste-bag dispensers, as well as the needed accessibility for maintenance equipment and vehicles. Having and keeping the maintenance workers in the loop throughout the project can prevent costly surprises and problems that are frequently unanticipated—these folks view the project differently than most others, and they can be extremely helpful with the planning and design process. Sometimes, the maintenance needs of a park project, unfortunately, may often be an afterthought, and the resulting problems could have been avoided.

The involvement of the maintenance employees also helps dispel fears, especially if the dog park concept is new in a community. For example, workers may worry that they will be the ones cleaning up after the dogs—this thought alone can certainly anger these folks and make them immediate adversaries of the project. Again, this can be avoided by including them and their input from day one.

Doing It Right

This is included here as a consideration because it is about an attitude. Since the concept is still a somewhat new one, particularly compared to traditional park venues such as sport fields and courts, swimming pools, and even picnic areas, few standards or even strong recommendations are available to refer to when initiating the development of a dog park. For example, most of the available material on the Internet is quite general, and it is often site specific. Much is simply about a particular community's experience creating and describing their own dog park. Some of this may be helpful, but some may be quite inappropriate, as related to climate, for example. Thus, research needs to be comprehensive enough to cover both the positives and negatives of others' experiences in creating dog parks (ideally, in the same geographic region) as well as to use basic, proven park principles that relate to the project. In order to optimize the potential success of the new community park venue, since they lack guidance to provide quality, helpful, appropriate information, so abundant for other park venues, those heading the project should be sincere, focused, and willing to devote the time and effort needed for developing the best dog park facility possible, within reasonable parameters. Winging it or simply copying the way a nearby community created their dog park (often including problems and all) is simply the wrong approach. Problems can relate to usage, rules, maintenance, costs, and so on. This is not the way to approach any new park project, but, because of the lack of information and expertise, creating a dog park is, understandably, more challenging.

That said, the attitude to do it right must prevail for all involved; from the community leaders to agency staff to maintenance employees to the volunteers, everyone should be on board to create the best dog park possible!

Of course, the last consideration previously mentioned, doing it right, is really the purpose of this book. With this attitude, all the other considerations listed should be viewed as steps to ultimately, indeed, do it right! Some of these considerations can often simply be checked off. If a proposed site is in an existing park, convenient appropriate parking may already be available. Check! Or, if the site is a new, unused, standalone property, there will be no proximity issues in relation to other park venues. Check! Agency maintenance employees are involved in the planning, meetings, and related discussions. Check!

Thus, as part of the process, these considerations are important and understandable, but they are often quite easy to evaluate. On the other hand, political, community, and financial support are examples of considerations that may need to be cultivated and nurtured to be able to move forward. This can take time and effort—meetings, discussions, educational endeavors, and some creativity may be needed. How about a field trip to a nearby dog park?

Those involved should be prepared to review and evaluate these considerations and the other steps necessary to ultimately create a dog park the community will be pleased with and proud of, and will happily and appropriately use.

Next, we begin to encounter and decide on the fun stuff! Chapter 4 covers the various components of a dog park. Though somewhat specific, these items offer many variables and commercial companies from which to choose. Communities often want to personalize their dog parks. This can be done through the various components, a color scheme, or a park theme. For some items, recommendations will be made, but for others, there may be a vast array of possibilities! In addition, some concerns will be noted and explained, especially in relation to items that are discouraged for the dog park.

So, get ready for the fun stuff! Pick colors, waste containers, and fountains, oh my!

Components

How does a space become a dog park? Find out which components you need to build your dog park right!

35

So, let's say an appropriate site has been selected. It has the needed support, and financing is falling into place. Now, exactly which elements do we need in the new space to create a dog park?

This chapter provides that important list, with descriptions and details about the needed elements that turn the selected site into a dog park. Some of the items may be natural features that need to be considered, or perhaps altered in some fashion, to become appropriate for a dog park. Other items will need to be purchased and installed. Some items may present fundraising opportunities that can lend themselves to the creation of a very personalized, unique, attractive, new community facility! See figure 4.1 for an example of what a dog park can look like when all these components come together.

Design and Natural Elements

Before listing and providing information about the various items, several aspects about the layout of the elected site must be discussed. This primarily concerns basic design and natural element options and considerations.

Configuration

The design of the space, which can be almost any configuration, must include three spaces: the transition or entry area, a large- or all-dog area, and a small-dog area. It is usually best to place the transition or entry enclosure on the outside of the two main fenced enclosures; this creates a separate section, typically placed with a main entry gate into the area and then one gate to enter the small-dog space and another to enter the large- or all-dog enclosure. It's also important to point out that 90-degree angles (and smaller) should always be avoided in the design and shape of the fenced enclosures; this helps prevent dogs from being cornered by other dogs, an experience which is upsetting to both owner and dog. The transition or entry space should be at least about 125 to 150 square feet (38–46 square m) in size. The all-dog area should be considerably larger than the small-dog area: two-thirds to three-fourths of the total space for large dogs and one-third to one-fourth of the total space for small dogs. The large- or all-dog area should certainly have a spacious, open expanse for the larger dogs to run and play, larger than a similar space for the small dogs. If the two main areas must be separated, rather than sharing a common section of fencing between them, then two transition or entry areas, one for each, must be created.

A new trend that should be mentioned here is creating a separate transition exit area. Though perhaps helpful for heavily used dog parks, it is probably not necessary for most and is an added expense.

If the space is large enough, say 2 or more acres, creating three large spaces may be desirable, so as to leave one space periodically unused for the turf to recover. This is typically done in high-use dog parks with grass or lawn-type surfacing. The spaces are then designated by shifting the signage (i.e., Large Dogs or All Dogs, Small Dogs, and Closed) from one space to another. If space

Figure 4.1 An example of a dog park layout.
© Doris Tomaselli | www.empresscreative.com

allows for these three fenced enclosures, they should all be large enough for large dogs, and thus somewhat similar in size.

Surfacing

This is often a huge concern. Numerous types of surfacing are used in off-leash areas, each with a number of advantages and disadvantages. No surfacing is perfect, but some variables and concerns should be taken into consideration.

I always prefer grass if at all possible. I *never* recommend wood chips or mulch. Sand is often an option frequently used in coastal or beach-oriented communities. Pea gravel is quite common as well. Another surface option, similar but superior to mulch or wood chips, is engineered wood fiber (EWF); this is the same surfacing material used in many children's playgrounds. Decomposed granite has, in some areas, become almost a standard dog park surfacing.

Other types of surfacing besides grass include (a) pea gravel, (b) mulch (wood chips) (c) sand, and (d) crushed aggregate.

Artificial turf, some currently made specifically for dog parks, is another option, but it is extremely expensive, even when used in very small off-leash areas.

Other important concerns here relate to climate and weather, topography, maintenance, amount and frequency of use, and disabled accessibility. These must be considered regardless of the surfacing type selected.

Table 4.1 indicates the advantages and disadvantages of each of the different types of surfacing commonly used in dog parks.

If a dog park, or an area within a dog park, is very sloped, almost all types of surfaces will experience problems. Though dog parks need not be level and some sloping can add interest, too much sloping can create an assortment of maintenance challenges, from erosion to containment issues to drainage problems and more.

As with all anticipated dog park maintenance concerns, maintenance staff should be involved with the surfacing discussions and decisions.

The topics of drainage and irrigation systems mentioned earlier may apply to some dog parks and may not be necessary in others. This is generally true of all types of parks throughout the country.

Determinations should be made in advance as to whether these types of site work are necessary. Especially for municipalities, professional municipal engineering staff may be able to make those recommendations. Understandably, these types of needs relate primarily to climate and weather.

Table 4.1 Surfacing Options for Dog Parks

Type of surfacing	Advantages	Disadvantages
Grass	Grass is attractive, accessible, and cost effective. In most areas, only regular mowing and periodic reseeding are needed. (Applies to creating a new dog park; in an existing park area, mowing may already be done regularly.) Grass is the most common form of turf for a dog park, and most users (dogs and people) prefer it. Often already exists. Even if grass deteriorates in some areas, letting it go to dirt may be acceptable.	Grass can die in high-traffic areas. Grass can become unattractive over time due to high traffic, weather, and urine. To minimize problems, the larger the park, the better. Another solution is to use hard surfaces (e.g., cement, see following) for the primary high-traffic areas. Finally, a section of a dog park can be closed to let the grass recover or 3 fenced enclosures could be created (vs. 2) to allow one area to be recovering while the others are in use. In some areas, grass without drainage or irrigation systems can become muddy and create puddles when it rains. Urine may be a problem, so urine-resistant grass is recommended.

> *continued*

Table 4.1 > *continued*

Type of surfacing	Advantages	Disadvantages
Mulch (wood chips)	Mulch is a popular turf, the second most common for dog parks, despite its many serious disadvantages. Mulch may absorb water from rainfall and minimize the creation of puddles. Mulch can work acceptably in climates with rain and snow.	Containment issues often occur with mulch. Mulch requires periodic raking and replenishment. Mulch may need to be watered periodically if rain has been minimal. Mulch can cost more than grass. The color and shape of the mulch makes it hard for people to see dogs' feces, which may cause them not to pick up after their dogs. Also, when difficult to see, both dogs and owners may step in feces. The bark contained in mulch can break down and decay; the decay can then infect the rest of the much. Since mulch can absorb liquids, including urine, it may emit an odor. Mulch can absorb bacteria and harbor parasites. Mulch can occasionally catch on fire. Mulch is usually not ADA accessible. Some dogs may chew or eat the mulch.
Engineered wood fiber (EWF)	EWF is accessible and often considered attractive. EWF is carefully controlled as to type and size of wood fibers. Usually, rain water can pass through EWF, which minimizes puddles and mud problems.	As with mulch, there are often containment issues. As with mulch, EWF requires periodic raking and replenishment. Sometimes, if not equipped with a drainage system, areas can become muddy and create puddles when it rains. The color and shape of EWF, similar to mulch, makes it hard for people to see dogs' feces, which may cause them not to pick up after their dogs. Also, when difficult to see, both dogs and owners may step in feces. EWF can be quite expensive, especially for an entire dog park.

Type of surfacing	Advantages	Disadvantages
Sand	Sand can be attractive, but is primarily used in beach-type communities (where it is plentiful). Sand is more commonly used as an amenity in dog parks (e.g., as a designated digging area).	Sand can absorb water, but can be sticky and messy when wet. Sand can have containment issues. Sand may need to be raked and replenished periodically. Sand is not ADA accessible.
Pea gravel	Pea gravel, a form of small, smooth, round rocks, allows water to drain and can work well in high-traffic areas. Pea gravel may be an alternative to grass in areas with minimal rainfall.	Some dogs may dislike the feeling of pea gravel on their paws, though they may get used to it over time. Pea gravel can have containment issues. It may need to be raked and replenished periodically. Pea gravel is not ADA accessible.
Decomposed granite (crushed aggregate)	Decomposed granite, also known as stone dust, is a very popular dog park surface in many areas. It is attractive and accessible. It packs well. Water drains through decomposed granite—it does not absorb water or urine. It is comfortable for dogs to walk on.	In some areas, without a drainage system, decomposed granite may get muddy, and puddles can form. It can create dust clouds. It may need to be watered periodically, especially if there is minimal rainfall. Decomposed granite may need replenishment over time. It can be expensive.
Artificial turf	Artificial turf can be an alternative to grass. Newer products may work well. It can work well in areas with minimal rainfall, as well as in areas with snow and more rain. Artificial turf is attractive, accessible, and long lasting.	Artificial turf is very expensive. It should be watered periodically, or it may develop an odor. It may need to have a drainage system.
Cement (and similar hardscape surfaces)	Cement should be primarily used for walkways, entrances, in the transitional areas, and under benches and entry aprons into the fenced enclosures—thus, it's good for high-traffic areas. It requires minimal maintenance. Cement enables park accessibility.	Cement can be unattractive (and inappropriate) if used as the surfacing for the entire dog park. It may get hot to the touch and be uncomfortable for dogs' feet.

Shade

In dog parks that do not have enough trees, structures that provide shade should be added.

Some dog park sites have adequate shade; many do not. Adequate shade basically means some amount of shade is available for both dogs and the dog owners. This is particularly important in warmer climates, but hot summer days are experienced virtually everywhere. Shade should be a site-selection consideration, however, a site without adequate shade (or no shade) need not be a problem. If a site does not provide appropriate natural shade from area trees, a variety of structures are available, often from companies that specialize in shade structures. Though natural shade is usually preferable, shade structures are often very attractive. They can be color coordinated and installed in specific, desirable areas of the park. They may be made of wood, metal, or other materials. Some are even made of fabric-type material, but all are designed for permanent outdoor applications. Again, however, whatever shade structures are considered, they must be designed for public, commercial applications from companies that provide their products to municipalities and various public places.

If the structures are to provide shade for dog owners, such as to cover benches, they should be installed around the perimeter of the fenced enclosures, where the benches should be placed. If they are to provide shade for the dogs, they can be installed almost anywhere in the enclosures, and should simply provide a shady space without creating visual obstructions. It's recommended that these structures be installed into hard surfaces for both aesthetics and ease of maintenance.

The size of the shade structures can vary greatly. The size selected may depend on the site size. Or, several structures may be selected. Each fenced enclosure should have some amount of shade. The large-dog or all-dog area may require a bigger shade structure or two shade structures, and the smaller space for the small dogs may have smaller structures or just one structure.

If natural shade is already available, it should be in each of the areas. If natural shade is more desirable in a community, trees can be planted. However, it is unlikely that a large enough tree can be planted to provide adequate shade immediately. Planting several trees, as well as installing some shade structures, could be a good initial compromise, with the intention of eventually removing the shade structures when the trees have grown large enough to provide an adequate amount of shade.

One last important point about planting trees in a dog park is that they must be protected. Stabilizing new trees and fencing them off prevents damage, especially from urine, and helps them get a good start in the dog park.

Structural Elements

This section discusses the important structures that essentially define the dog park facility space, especially identifying the perimeter needs. I am referring first, of course, to the fencing, which is perhaps the most important structural element of a dog park and, most assuredly, the most expensive. In addition, this section explains the hardscape needs, which also tend to be mostly in perimeter areas of the dog park.

Fencing and Gates

The fencing is perhaps, understandably, the most important dog park component and the most expensive aspect of the facility (including both materials and labor). Most of the time, chain link is used. I always suggest the black,

If chain link is selected for the fencing, it should be the type that is coated in black vinyl—it tends to blend into the background better and is more aesthetically appealing.

The fence should be at least 5 feet (1.5 m) high and should include top and bottom rails.

The size, type, and location of maintenance gates should be determined with the assistance and input of employees who will be responsible for the maintenance tasks.

vinyl-coated type. Black blends in best with the background, creating a far less visible enclosure. Other fencing materials available are satisfactory, but chain link seems to be the most cost efficient; it is usually already in use in an existing park, it is sturdy and reliable, and it usually has a long life. The fence should include both top and bottom rails, with the bottom rails installed as close to the ground as possible. The fence should be a minimum of 5 feet (1.5 m) in height.

When installing the fencing, if a portion of the dog park is along a wooded area, the fencing can be pulled slightly inside the woods line, 5 to 10 feet (1.5–3 m), as long as visibility for monitoring dogs isn't affected (depending on the thickness or type of woods, shrubs, and so on). This can be visually appealing, and it creates more interest for the dogs and can make mowing and maintenance somewhat easier.

Several gates will be needed: main exterior gates for the transition entry areas, interior gates off the transition areas or entries going into the enclosures, and maintenance gates, which are usually doubled or larger than the other gates, with their location determined with the assistance of maintenance employees. The two sets of gates needed for the transition areas or entries should be self-latching, with both opening toward the interior spaces. These gates should also be wide enough to be ADA compliant, especially for dog owners who use wheelchairs.

Hardscape Surfaces

Hard surfaces are mentioned in this chapter in conjunction with a number of other components. Seating areas, fountains, and shade structures all need hard surfaces below them, but the waste-bag dispensers or stations, especially if installed on posts, can have hard-surface bases as well. Even the waste cans can be placed on hard surfaces. This all makes the surface maintenance easier (especially if it is natural turf), faster, more convenient, and more efficient. However, I also always recommend a hardscape surface for the transition areas

Ideally, all equipment and amenities located throughout a dog park should be placed on a hard surface, primarily for ease of maintenance.

or entrances, as well as a large swath of hard surface for an apron just beyond the transition area enclosure, always an area of very high traffic within the main fenced enclosures. That means a hard surface at least 10 to 15 feet (3–4.5 m) beyond the transition area or entrance. If this is not done, regardless of the type of surface used for the rest of the dog park, this space becomes very messy. Grass is destroyed and other materials become depleted. Bare ground will create mud and exposed pebbles, rocks, or roots that may be problematic for both people and dogs. Placing a hardscape surface in this area prevents those problems and provides a very attractive, clean look to the dog park entrance. The

Any type of hardscape apron in a dog park entry area will help preserve the adjacent grass surfacing, since the entry generally receives more wear and tear than any other area in the park.

hard-surface apron should be large enough to go to at least some of the perimeter fencing so that someone in a wheelchair can easily use it. An owner using a wheelchair can thus easily come into the dog park through the transition area or entrance and then place themselves just inside the fenced enclosure, still on the hard surface, to supervise their dog.

It's important to mention, at this point, the desirability of using some type of bricks or pavers in the entry areas described previously. These provide an attractive look on entering the facility as an alternative to simple hard surfacing. For communities involved with fundraising to finance all or part of their dog park's development costs, I often recommend that the park's entry area use a

Bricks should be used in the entry area when possible to enhance the park's aesthetic.

A hard-surface walkway in the dog park provides the opportunity for walking, as well as greater accessibility.

fundraising bricks program. Supporters make a contribution that includes the purchase of a brick that will be permanently engraved with the purchaser's sentiment, usually honoring or memorializing someone, often a pet. The bricks are then installed in a surface area of the dog park, often in the transition or entry areas. These bricks have become a very popular type of fundraising program, and they provide a perfect application for the entry area's hard surfaces—far more attractive than the pavement or cement. They also create a personalized community identity for the dog park and its supporters.

Occasionally, a hard-surface path may also be created, usually just inside along the perimeter of the fenced enclosures, particularly in larger dog parks. This is essentially a walking path that owners may use for themselves as exercise while they continue to supervise their dogs and to encourage their dogs to walk or exercise as they follow the path. It is also a means for people using wheelchairs or walkers to access more central areas of the dog park's fenced enclosures. This is a nice-to-have feature in which a community may or may not be interested. A hard-surface path, can, of course, be added in the future, if desired.

Equipment

This section identifies the essential items that a dog park must have. However, it also mentions optional items that dog parks may have, but which are not necessary or required for a quality dog park facility. For most of the basic items, many manufacturers are available that can offer a wide variety of products that will meet the needs of any community, in many colors, styles, designs, and prices.

Benches

There are *many* types of benches to choose from! The community may already use a particular type, so maintaining that uniformity makes sense. However, if the dog park is to be unique as to style, color, design features, and so on, certainly, the sky's the limit when selecting benches! Some guidelines are in order here: Benches should always be selected that are meant for a commercial, public park application, never those designed for residential use. Communicate with appropriate companies that regularly supply benches for use in public places. They can provide a wealth of information as to the advantages and disadvantages of the various types, construction, longevity, finishes, vandalism resistance, weather or climate

Many different types of commercial park benches are available for park facilities, including dog parks. Since some agencies have a particular type used in all their parks for a uniform look, the benches for their dog park can certainly be selected to maintain that consistency.

concerns, mounts (whether in the ground, surface, or portable), costs, and so on.

Some benches come with a roof-type structure for shade, some have arms, some may get hot in direct sun, and some may occasionally need replacement parts—all these are variables to consider. There are now benches available specifically with dog parks in mind. They usually feature paw prints or dog bone designs and appear particularly appropriate for a dog park.

Bench placement is another component concern. Benches should always be placed around the interior of the perimeter facing in. This facilitates easy owner supervision of dogs from anywhere in the fenced enclosures. If benches are to be placed or installed under a shade structure or gazebo, the structure should be placed closer to a perimeter location than toward the middle of the enclosure, and the benches underneath should face toward the middle or center area of the enclosure. Again, the orientation of the benches should always maximize the viewing area for owners' supervision of their dogs.

The benches should be installed in, and surrounded by, a hard surface. This provides for an attractive installation as well as for ease of maintenance.

Placing two or three benches next to one another in several places in the dog park is very desirable, in addition to arranging single benches here and there. The hard surface recommended below the benches, when there are two or three in a row, can be done as one elongated hard-surface pad, thus making turf maintenance even easier.

It is important to have an adequate number of benches in a dog park. This encourages comfortable, convenient usage of the facility. as well as fostering the dog park's social benefits for the dog owners. Without adequate seating areas, a number of possible negative ramifications may occur. For example, people may simply not be interested in using the park if there is no place to sit. Or, they may bring a variety of personal inexpensive outdoor chairs and leave them in the park. More often than not, these seats are in poor condition, often dirty or even damaged. They can create a hazardous situation in relation to safety and liability for a community, not to mention the poor visual perception of a haphazard assortment of old, unattractive, dirty, cheap chairs. Thus, an adequate number of quality park benches is certainly an important component of a dog park.

Only simple park-type benches should be used for seating in dog parks, never picnic tables! Picnic tables encourage owners to sit and face each other, thus ignoring their dogs, or they may eat, drink, or smoke—all inappropriate activities in a dog park. Dogs also may climb up on picnic tables, and owners may encourage this behavior! Even benches or picnic tables outside the fenced enclosures can be problematic, encouraging owners to leave their dogs inside the fenced area while they go outside the enclosures for whatever reason.

Fountains

A water line or connection for a dog water fountain is a must! Dog parks should not be created without a fountain. Users will bring water in various types of containers, as well as bring water bowls of every type imaginable. Typically, these things are left in the dog park. This also creates mud and dirty water everywhere, and the park quickly resembles a pig pen, which is unattractive, messy, and often unhealthy.

I usually recommend that the fountains be of the type that offer four features: the pet fountain at the base, two people fountains at the top (regular height and lower height for people using wheelchairs), and, ideally, a separate, lockable bib attachment providing a water spigot, which may come in handy and isn't a very expensive additional option. A hand-wash attachment is another optional feature some may want to consider. For northern locations, I usually recommend the type of fountains that will provide water only in warmer weather, not in the winter. Those are far more expensive, and I don't feel they are necessary, but they are certainly an option. Several companies provide the various types of fountain units indicated here, including the optional features mentioned as well as other options communities may want to consider. They are available in a variety of colors, finishes, and textures (often providing graffiti resistance).

Some dog parks, especially in southern locations, also offer dog-wash stations in the dog park vicinity. The fountain companies may be able to assist with this equipment as well. Again, it's important that the fountain companies provide their equipment for commercial, public parks or locations. They will also provide, if necessary, installation information, which is typically handled by a local plumber or appropriate, qualified maintenance employee.

A fountain should be installed in each of the two fenced enclosures.

A wide variety of types of water fountains exist, but most will include at least one fountain for people and one for dogs.

A dog-wash station can be a nice feature in warmer climates.

If, however, there's just one transition or entry area, with gates opening to each of the fenced enclosures, one fountain inside the transition area would be acceptable. That means the owners will have to bring their dogs into the transition area or entrance to get a drink. This shouldn't be a problem, but it's more desirable to have two separate fountains, one in each enclosure. Often, the two fountains can be installed directly across from one another in the two areas with the shared fence in between. However, since dogs may try to mark the fountain, it may be better located in the transition entry area where an owner's presence may discourage this behavior.

The fountains will need appropriate drainage. As with the benches, a hard surface surrounding the fountain is recommended for both aesthetics and easy maintenance.

Waste-Bag Stations

Waste bags must be provided in dog parks for owners to fulfill perhaps the most important self-policing requirement in a dog park. If feces wasn't picked up and disposed of consistently by the dogs' owners, as a serious, important priority, dog parks probably wouldn't exist. This responsibility is absolutely mandatory for dog parks to be successful. Thus, the community must provide these bags in a convenient, efficient manner and must take their responsibility to do so very seriously, for the benefit of all. This is only one of a handful of responsibilities that will be required by the community to maintain the dog park they are developing. That means selecting a waste-bag provider, usually obtaining and placing several waste-bag distribution stations (at least one in each fenced area as well as one in the transition or entry area) in the dog park, and monitoring the dispensers to make sure bags are always available for the dog owners. Some waste-bag companies send out cases of the bags on a regular basis to the community agencies, but the dispensers must, of course, be filled manually.

Currently, many different types of waste bags and waste-bag dispenser stations are available from numerous companies. Most offer some type of plastic, biodegradable bag, provided on a roll or from a card for one-at-a-time dispensing. There are a variety of types of dispensers and stations, most of which are usually mounted on a post. The stations can often be customized with the name of the dog park or the agency. In some cases, the bags can be personalized as well (though that seems a bit silly and unnecessary).

When determining which type of waste bags, dispensers, and stations you will use in a dog park, you must consider the number and placement of the dispensers or stations. There should always be a dispenser or station in the transition entry, for example. This way, owners can take a bag into the fenced enclosure on their way in—a behavior that should always be encouraged! Usually, at least one additional dispenser or station should be placed in each fenced area, depending on the size, layout, and the proximity or relationship to maintenance access. Larger dog parks may have many such units, instead of just two or three. Lastly, the dispensers or stations should always be placed near the perimeter fencing, not far from bench areas.

A final note should be included about septic systems for dog parks. I have heard that there are such systems in some dog parks, but there is a lack of quality information about them. I suspect they may be residential systems installed

You'll have a wide variety of types to choose from when selecting waste-bag stations.

in dog parks that may or may not be appropriate or work well. Though it is possible they may become a feature of dog parks in the future, I believe a commercial system would need to be developed.

Covered Waste Cans

These are often provided by the same companies that supply waste bags, dispensers, and stations. Frequently, they are actually part of a station setup with the waste cans attached to posts. However, those attached waste cans are usually quite small and may be inadequate for high-traffic dog parks, since frequent emptying may be a problem. Thus, I often don't recommend the all-in-one waste station setups.

Regardless of the type, waste cans in a dog park must close tightly and securely, and they should allow for easy emptying by maintenance workers.

In many communities, a waste can with a particular type, size, and color is used throughout their parks and public or commercial areas for a uniform look. There's no reason those same waste cans can't be used in a community's new dog park, as long as they have securely closing lids. Maintaining a particular look or color scheme throughout a community's park system can usually provide a positive branding effect. Or, some type of new waste cans can be obtained for the new facility. Guidelines here begin with selecting waste cans with covers that securely and tightly close. At the same time, they must be easy to empty, usually using interior liners. These aspects of proper dog park waste receptacles relate to cleanliness, health, odor, ease of maintenance, and even attractiveness. Frankly, everything relating to waste in a dog park must be considered a top priority. Some heavy-duty waste cans are available specifically for dog park applications that are particularly good choices. One concern some users have, however, is that they prefer not to have to touch the waste can. This can render an issue in relation to waste-can covers that close tightly, since those usually involve the need for manual touching. Some dog park waste cans simply provide an open hole to deposit the used bags in, with no cover at all. My priority here is a concern about odor, but some community members may feel it is more important not to have to touch the waste can at all. When selecting the waste cans for the dog park, the maintenance employees who will be responsible for collection and emptying waste should be included in the discussions. In addition, those discussions should include decisions concerning the number and location of the waste cans in the fenced enclosures. For example, just as waste-bag dispensers or stations should be placed in the transition and entry areas for users as they enter the fenced enclosures, waste cans, too, should be located there. Other locations for waste cans in the fenced enclosures should be convenient for pickup and should not be too close to seating areas.

Signage

This is an important component of a dog park, especially in areas where dog parks are still considered a new concept. The park should have at least two signs and, ideally, a bulletin board.

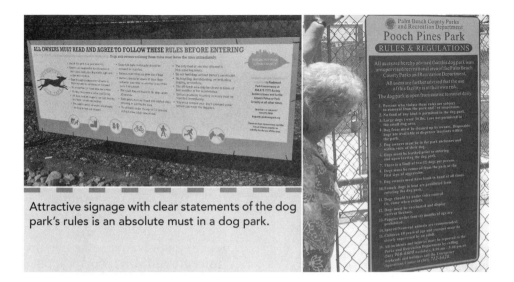

Attractive signage with clear statements of the dog park's rules is an absolute must in a dog park.

One sign should indicate the name of the dog park, even if located within an existing park. It should be somewhat large and professionally made, and should have a welcoming feel as to attractiveness, color, font style, and so on. If the community already has a uniform signage program, the dog park sign should be appropriately matched, exhibiting that it fits in with the community's established tradition. This sign should, of course, be located near the dog park entrance. If the dog park is in a particular area some distance from an existing park's main entry, it may be necessary to first provide some ancillary directional signage near the park's main entrance, pointing patrons toward the dog park.

The dog park must have a sign containing the full list of its rules. As with all park rules, this should not simply be a list of don'ts—it should instead be a comprehensive listing of the requirements that enable the dog park to operate safely and fairly for all users, including the important emphasis of self-enforcement. The use of terms such as *please* and phrases such as "for everyone's benefit" should be used liberally. This conveys a positive, equitable, friendly tone instead of a list of what not to do. In addition, this sign should indicate traditional information that users often seek, in addition to the rules. This may include dog park hours, the municipality's hold harmless clause, emergency contact information, and often a statement like "Please leave our dog park nicer than you found it." Suggested rules are discussed in chapter 6.

A bulletin board, designed for permanent outdoor use, is always an important feature at a dog park. It can be used to display fliers, announcements, community information, the availability of various dog-related classes, programs or events, and so on. Dog park users may also appreciate the opportunity to place lost and found alerts on the board or perhaps to sell dog-related items. This fairly standard dog park component is appreciated by all.

Additional signs are usually not necessary throughout the dog park. Even a few extra signs can make a dog park appear cluttered. Some dog parks use additional signage as reminders for owners to pick up after their dogs. This may be necessary and desirable, especially in larger fenced enclosures. After all, the

A bulletin board provides a place for dog park users to share and learn about information relevant to them.

Smaller signs can be useful reminders of key rules, especially in a larger dog park, but take care not to create a cluttered appearance.

importance of owners picking up after their dogs cannot be stressed enough. Some communities have even placed these reminder signs outside the fenced enclosures to provide additional emphasis in the general vicinity of the dog park. Often, too, reminders are preprinted on dog-waste stations.

Homemade signage of any type should be discouraged in the dog park. Also, posters, announcements, and so on to be placed on the enclosed bulletin board should require approval in some manner from an appropriate person, policy body, or the parks agency.

Optional Equipment

Some dog parks contain items or equipment that are not necessary, but are often considered desirable or even needed by particular members of a community. Some items may even reflect the nature or characteristics of a community.

Fire Hydrant

Perhaps the most common and comical of these extra items is a fire hydrant placed in the fenced enclosures. Many municipalities have older hydrants no longer being used that can be appropriately repurposed in a dog park. Often, they are repainted in the dog park's color theme (or in some other manner), and they become an interesting, bright focal point, especially for the male dogs.

Art and Sculpture

Some simple sculpture-type items are also commercially available, and some are specifically designed for dog parks. These are often large, low pieces that dogs can

Homemade signs create an unprofessional aesthetic when posted on park fences.

climb on. They often depict dogs, cats, and other animals. Again, these types of items are not necessary, but they can be attractive additions to a dog park.

Some communities may want to emphasize their artistic priorities. They may want to incorporate art or sculpture in some way in their dog park. This has been done quite magnificently in some places. However, the art, in whatever form, should be created for a public, outdoor, permanent application. It should also be of safe materials and a design that will not harm either dogs or people—no sharp edges, dangerous finishes (dogs might be attracted to chew or lick), or insecure installation (especially if the item is heavy or precariously balanced). A good dose of common sense should apply here in relation to safety. Some dog parks have been created with numerous objets d'art. This is especially true in communities known for their artistic populations. Dog parks in communities like these can become tourist destinations, since they offer interesting, attractive, unusual exhibits in an unexpected locale. These communities are proud to present their unique dog parks to the public, reflecting the artistic character of their residents.

As a cautionary note, I must mention the undesirability of homemade items and structures by well-meaning but nonprofessional people. Most of these types of dog park additions may look attractive initially, but they quickly become eyesores as they deteriorate and become faded and damaged by the elements. They often become dangerous as well, with problems such as exposed nails or broken, sharp pieces of wood. In other words, these homemade additions are virtually always problematic, and they typically, eventually, look awful. They can render an otherwise well-designed dog park facility unattractive, shoddy, and even dangerous.

Fire hydrants are always fun in a dog park. Sometimes they are painted to reflect their repurposing, as the spotted one and the Stan Laurel here.

Agility Equipment

Speaking of additions, community members often want to include agility equipment in a dog park. Some of these folks are interested in this because they are knowledgeable canine-agility enthusiasts, while others simply feel the equipment would be nice to have. I usually recommend the following when this topic arises: For those serious agility folks, if agility training equipment is a must have, it would be more appropriately placed in a separate, fenced enclosure, with permanently installed quality equipment, than in the community dog park. If this is not possible, then portable agility equipment may be a possibility. Again, the equipment should be heavy duty and of professional quality instead of homemade. In addition, providing a nearby, well-secured storage shed would help the agility enthusiasts, especially if they raise funds for the shed themselves. A bonus of agility equipment is that agility demonstrations and lessons can provide wonderful program and event opportunities for a community's recreation and park's activity offerings.

Playground Equipment

Several companies now provide playground equipment specifically for dog parks. The pieces are colorful, whimsical, and attractive. Some are professionally manufactured, not terribly different from commercial children's playground equipment. For the most part, they are safe.

As attractive and fun as it is to see agility equipment or playground pieces in a dog park, I must discuss a few cautionary points. First, the equipment often

Agility equipment and playground pieces can be nice additions to a dog park, as long as they are designed for outdoor, heavy-duty use.

does look like traditional playground equipment, and children tend to be more attracted to the pieces than dogs are. The equipment is not designed for children and thus, understandably, it may not hold up as well as may be expected when children use it. The equipment, especially the better quality pieces for dog park play, is usually expensive. With so many communities struggling for funding to

Art or sculpture in a dog park setting, as long as they are heavy duty, able to withstand extreme weather, and low maintenance, can be a creative, attractive, interesting addition.

create their first dog park, providing play equipment is quite unnecessary. On the other hand, many may find the available equipment quite desirable and want to include it in the design of their dog park. Since this equipment is quite showy compared to items such as the fencing and waste cans, it is certainly possible that folks might be willing to donate the costs for canine off-leash playground equipment. However, providing play equipment should never take priority over the essential required components needed for developing a quality dog park.

One final comment about dog park agility and playground equipment relates again to quality, commercial applications. This concern must not be minimized—from several perspectives. These types of items placed in a dog park must be safe, appropriately manufactured, heavy duty, installed properly and securely, maintained as needed and recommended, and designed for an outdoor, commercial, public application (i.e., they should never be residential or homemade pieces).

Security Systems

Though I greatly prefer that dog parks be open to public usage similar to park playgrounds, picnic areas, play fields, and the like, some communities prefer to limit access to their dog parks to their own residents or members, who must often pay a fee. Then, typically, the user is provided with a way to access the dog park that nonresidents or those who haven't paid cannot use. Sometimes, it may be a tag of some type attached to the member's dog's collar, a sticker on the member's car, or a special key. However, more technological approaches may involve swiping an access card, or QR (quick response) code systems may even be used. Many security companies and locksmiths can provide security systems and equipment that can accommodate communities with these needs.

It's important to point out, though, that most of the security systems and needed equipment are not foolproof, and many communities have had problems. It's difficult, for example, to keep users from allowing guests (nonmembers), often with their dogs, into the dog park when they access it.

In addition, costs are involved in administering fees and memberships, as well as with the related enforcement needs. This is in addition to the cost of the security equipment. In some cases, especially where low fees are preferred and encouraged (by the powers that be), the costs may exceed the minimal revenue!

Dog Aquatics

This topic may or may not be broached when a community begins considering a dog park project. Though some communities have swimming pool facilities, there doesn't appear to be a consensus on how best to create and maintain them for dogs.

Many feel the opportunity for dogs to enjoy water is an important consideration. Swimming also has a therapeutic benefit for dogs, not dissimilar to those for people.

Parks may have access to man-made bodies of water, as well as to ponds and beaches. Various types of encounters with wildlife are not uncommon—examples include fish, ducks, turtles, snakes, frogs, and even creatures such as jellyfish. Most of these encounters may not be problematic, but dogs can certainly be injured by a snake, jellyfish, or snapping turtle.

Municipal water is often used for some of these bodies of water, and the Board of Health usually requires the same vaccinations that all dog parks should require.

Pools or bodies of water in dog parks should be enclosed separately to allow owners to decide whether they want their dogs to go into the water. For some, a wet dog in their cars afterwards may be undesirable. Thus, the design of the dog park should allow for usage both with and without access to the water. Dog beaches are usually not traditional enclosed facilities, but rather opportunities for dogs to enjoy a community's natural resources, usually off leash—a truly wonderful community offering, but without the safety and protection of an enclosed space.

Creating a body of water in a dog park should involve appropriate aquatic professionals. They should be presented with all the information necessary as to the similarities and differences between the needs for a dog park and a traditional aquatic facility for people. As always, maintenance needs must be considered, along with the design and construction determinations.

So, we've covered both the must-have elements of a dog park and the nice-to-have elements. To briefly review, the truly necessary components include the appropriate surfacing material for the majority of the park, shade, fencing (including gates), specific hardscape surface areas, benches, dog and people fountains, waste-bag stations, covered waste cans, and appropriate signage. All other items mentioned are truly optional and not needed, though some supporters may feel they are desirable amenities and may endeavor to seek additional funding or donors for the items.

So we're now off to the next chapter to discuss landscaping and maintenance. Landscaping and the hardscape areas, along with appropriate signage, should have an aesthetic, inviting look that says, "C'mon in! This place is really nice! You're gonna like it in here—especially you, Rover!" These aspects of the dog park need not be extensive; a simple, attractive, clean, safe, welcoming appearance will do the trick!

Dog park maintenance needs, perhaps surprisingly for some, are really quite minimal, especially compared to those of many other park venues and facilities. Plus, when created in an existing community park, much of the required maintenance for the dog park is already being performed on a regular basis!

So, we're off to growing and mowing!

5

Landscaping and Maintenance

Little effort is needed to keep the dog park in good shape. Find out how to maximize your park's aesthetics and appeal, making it attractive and user friendly for all!

As with *any* park, landscaping and maintenance are facts of life. How these responsibilities are carried out can clearly indicate the difference between an agency headed by professional parks and recreation administrators and an agency that is often not professionally managed. These responsibilities are certainly important, but, in most cases, they are quite simple and straightforward.

So what exactly is involved in maintaining a dog park? This is a very common and understandable question that typically comes up at informational presentations where most attendees are encountering the concept of dog parks for the first time. I'll answer, initially, by pointing out what is *not* part of the agency's maintenance responsibilities: Agency maintenance staff is not involved in picking up feces in the dog park! Though it has already been mentioned several times, this extremely important responsibility (very possibly viewed as the most important dog park responsibility) belongs to dog owners, period. Again, it is most assuredly not the responsibility of anyone else. Those new to the concept of dog parks, both residents and municipal employees, especially parks maintenance staff, must hear and understand this up front. Thus, this simply must be made clear, here, right at the very beginning of this chapter. Now we can move forward.

Landscaping

This topic primarily refers to the entry of a dog park, actually just outside of the facility. That is often the only location where an attractive use of trees, shrubs, or flowers ought to greet park users. However, as described in chapter 4, I strongly recommend hardscaped areas throughout a dog park, which should be considered in this section.

When referring to the landscaping of the entry area, I'm primarily concerned with a minimal amount of plants to simply dress up the entrance and with the signage of the facility to welcome the users. Realistically, I believe that *any* park should have this minimal amenity to provide an attractive, warm, welcoming impression when entering. The plantings selected should be low maintenance, and maintenance employees should provide input. A few well-placed shrubs, even if just around the base of the sign showing the name of the dog park, can make a positive difference in the aesthetics of a new park facility, especially in relation to first impressions. If other locations are appropriate for some attractive plantings around the exterior of the dog park, by all means, go ahead! This is recommended, since it will contribute to the overall positive aesthetic of the park. Examples of these other locations for some landscaping near the dog park might be in relation to the parking area, nearby storage buildings or restrooms, or by additional park signs or bulletin boards.

Often, a local garden club is interested in providing assistance with these types of landscape planting projects, but make sure that these areas are easy to maintain, requiring only infrequent attention. Of course, if the volunteering club (or other organization) is also willing to maintain what they've created, that should be welcomed. However, an agency supervisor should make sure that they have periodic contact with the club to ensure appropriate, regular follow-through.

Since all public parks should provide professionally made entry signs, including some minimal, low-maintenance landscaping can add aesthetic appeal. It should be considered an important, yet inexpensive, additional welcoming feature for a community's new dog park.

Hopefully, the hardscape areas will be installed professionally and will need very minimal maintenance. These primarily include the hard surfaces inside the transition entry, the apron at the entrance of fenced enclosures, surfaces under the benches, water fountains, and shade structures, plus any pathways created in or around the dog park. Whether they are made of pavement, bricks, or some type of pavers, these areas should be kept in good repair, without weeds or other problems. However, minimal maintenance should be needed. With just a little attention periodically, these hardscape locations in the dog park are part of the simple attractiveness of the facility. Along with several well-placed shrubs, trees, and perhaps some flowers, the overall attractive appearance of the dog park makes a positive statement about the community and its attitude about the importance and value of its parks in general and its dog park in particular.

Maintenance

Though this has already been referred to in several venues, and most dog park upkeep is fairly minimal, maintenance is still important. It must be considered whenever a dog park project is being discussed. This, of course, is true of *any* park facility project.

Also, as mentioned several times, input from maintenance staff is crucial. It must be considered from the very beginning. These folks view the project differently than anyone else, and they are the ones ultimately responsible for its upkeep. Their often creative input can be extremely helpful and can even reflect cost savings—in relation to the initial creation of the facility as well as to their maintenance role. I can't emphasize the importance of their inclusion enough.

So, what exactly does the maintenance of a dog park entail? Let's begin with the basics of park maintenance. Emptying waste cans and removing garbage comes to mind first. Maintenance crews must do this regularly in all parks.

Overgrowth of vines should not be permitted to occur. Periodic maintenance along fencing is needed for prevention.

This responsibility is no different in a dog park, though the nature of the garbage is different. Thus, maintaining the pick-up schedule might have a bit more urgency. Hopefully, the type of waste cans and lids selected will prevent odor, but if the schedule is not maintained properly, especially if the cans are allowed to overflow, the agency can count on a much greater likelihood of complaints from the dog park folks than from users at other park facilities with a similar problem.

The next maintenance basic that applies to dog parks is mowing, assuming, of course, that the surfacing is grass. Again, including parks staff in the planning stage of a dog park project can make this chore much easier. Mowing the dog park should also be on the crew's regular maintenance schedule, as with trash removal. However, there is some flexibility here compared with, for example, a soccer field or a ball field. Mowing athletic fields are simply a higher priority and are possibly a liability concern. Never-

Damaged components must be repaired as soon as possible in order to keep the dog park safe for users and visually appealing.

theless, maintaining an appropriate mowing schedule for the community dog park is important for ensuring the facility looks good, which makes it easier for users to pick up after their dogs and reflects the agency's positive attitude about properly maintaining their parks for the benefit of all.

Keeping the dog park both safe and attractive for all users may also mean periodically clearing brush and trimming the overgrowth of weeds and ivy-type plants. Mowing or weed whacking may take care of these, but more work may be necessary in some cases. Though this overgrowth may occur anywhere in the dog park, it is frequently found around the base of trees or in and around the fencing. Poison ivy and the like are of particular concern, and they should be removed entirely.

Repairs, perhaps in relation to the fencing, hard surfaces, signage, benches, and so on would be the next common responsibility. Things break or get damaged or vandalized—these are simple realities in recreation and parks. Sometimes the damage is simple wear and tear, but sometimes, unfortunately, it's malicious. I always feel wear and tear is a good thing—it shows that a facility is truly being used, and that's why it was created. However, these problems must be addressed and resolved in a timely manner by the maintenance staff. Sometimes, they must recognize the need for repair and arrange for others to come do the work. If, for example, there's a problem with the water fountain, a plumber may need to be contacted. Regardless of the repair required, these types of problems require timely attention, again, as with any park facility.

Many people, especially in the northern regions of the United States, when first broaching the idea of a community dog park, inquire about what happens with dog parks during winter weather, especially snow. Perhaps surprisingly for some, the answer is that, usually, folks still use the dog park! So, what does that mean for the maintenance personnel? It means that at least some snow removal should be done in the parking area to the dog park. The walkway between the parking area and the transitional entry area should be cleared as well. Users basically just need access to the fenced enclosures. More intervention than that, say clearing snow from benches, really isn't necessary. Of course, regular responsibilities, such as garbage pickup, continue year-round. In many cases, however, the scheduled frequency of some tasks may change with the seasons.

In the northern climates, I always suggest that water fountains be shut down for the winter season. Fountains designed to be turned off in the winter are far less expensive, and the water requirement I advocate is primarily aimed at warmer weather periods. Fountains that can be used year-round, including through cold winters, are available.

Now, some maintenance concerns specifically relate to dog park needs. The first of these is making sure the waste stations always have waste bags available. Regular refilling of the stations is key to enforcing that all-important rule that owners must pick up after their dogs. Maintenance staff should do all they can to make sure the waste stations never run out—if that happens, the ramifications can be far worse than just not having waste bags available, which, of course, is not a problem you want your users to encounter and have to deal with. Empty waste stations can make users think that the agency really doesn't care that much about the dog park operating correctly; that keeping these things filled just isn't a priority for maintenance workers; it's OK to not pick up after their dog this one time; or they should bring their own bags! These are *not* messages you want the public to even think about. Once usage needs are determined (that is, how many bags, on average, a particular dog park uses), some waste-bag companies can automatically provide your agency with the needed number of bags on a regular basis. This is a convenient service, but the bags still must be taken to the dog park and the station units refilled.

Occasionally, repairs are needed in a dog park that may or may not be similar to upkeep needs in other parks. This can relate to the fencing, the water fountain, a bench, a gate mechanism, and so on. As much as I encourage the rule that dogs should be discouraged from digging holes and owners must fill any holes their dogs dig, this can be an ongoing problem, since the same holes may be dug again and again. Maintenance staff may be needed to provide a more professional refilling to solve the problem. The key here, however, is that the maintenance needs for every type of park will include the most common of park responsibilities, as well as various nuances of tasks specific to the particular park. Sometimes, especially at first, it may be more about attitude than anything else. So, yet again, I'll emphasize including parks employees in the dog park planning from the beginning.

Finally, when the dog park isn't covered with grass, surfacing maintenance must be realized and taken seriously. Whether the surfacing is sand, pea gravel, decomposed granite, engineered wood fiber, or mulch (I hope not!), these surfaces must be periodically replenished and raked to keep them in good condition. I have seen many dog parks where this is not done as it should be, and they look terrible. Once a dog park facility begins to look messy, it deteriorates quickly and soon looks even worse. Users will feel that the agency doesn't care about the park, and bad attitudes quickly follow, such as "It doesn't matter if I pick up after my dog or not," "I don't have to follow the rules," and "Who cares if I leave litter?" Thus, it is extremely important to keep the surfaces in good condition and replenished, clean, and raked. One other note here: These responsibilities should never be designated to volunteers. They are public park responsibilities that should be handled by the park or agency's maintenance employees on a regular basis. The volunteer groups that often initiate a dog park project are frequently so enthusiastic about the prospect of getting a community dog park that they will quickly say they are willing to take on many responsibilities just to make it happen. As wonderful as that enthusiasm is, dog park maintenance responsibilities, like maintenance responsibilities for *any* park, belong in the realm of agency staff. This may mean professional park employees. As should be expected, the dog park responsibilities become a regular part of their scheduled tasks. Well-meaning volunteers come and go. Some may move away, change their schedules, or eventually develop different priorities, and so on. Making a volunteer commit to maintaining a park just isn't realistic, especially in the long term. It simply isn't their job nor should it be!

So now we've covered the issue of what to do about maintenance. Mostly mowing, tending, emptying, and filling. Truly, as I indicated at the beginning of this chapter, these tasks are not difficult, complicated, or intensive. Still, they are certainly important in a community dog park, and attitude and consistency often become the priorities for a job well done.

Now, we move on to chapter 6 for dog park rules and etiquette. We've covered lots of the how-tos from the dog park agency's perspective, now we get to the how-to from the user's perspective!

Dog Park Rules and Etiquette

6

Your dog park will bring together all kinds of people and dogs in one place! Learn how to establish rules and guidelines that will bring out the best behavior in everyone.

Dog parks work because, for the most part, users follow the rules. This important aspect of a well-functioning dog park cannot be emphasized enough, since the overwhelming majority of dog parks involve self-enforcement of the rules. Staffing, or even periodic supervision by any type of authority, is minimal at best, and is often nearly nonexistent. Thus, for a dog park to maintain its operation in a safe, appropriate manner, ideally with few problems, users simply must monitor their dogs' behavior, as well as their own.

This chapter identifies and explains the various most-recommended rules that govern the operation of most dog parks. Following that is a discussion of dog park etiquette, which is primarily about human conduct in a dog park that can enhance the dog park experience and, perhaps more importantly, minimize problems. This includes identifying and explaining strategies to avoid conflicts and resolve issues. Since most rules in a dog park are usually self-enforced, with no person in charge, users take on the responsibility, whether they realize it or not, of enabling their dog park to run as it should—safely, efficiently, and correctly, with both dogs and their owners behaving properly for the benefit of all.

Mandatory Rules

Some rules must be adopted in any dog park, no matter the location or type or context. Let's consider the basic rules that keep dog parks safe and clean for everyone.

Clean Up Waste

> Owners must clean up after their dogs and dispose of it in provided waste containers.

Often it seems this is considered the most important dog park rule. It is the one that most concerns people new to the concept of dog parks. In other words, it's about picking up and disposing of your dog's feces. Indeed, this is, most assuredly, an absolutely essential rule that can certainly make or break a dog park. As mentioned previously, both waste bags and appropriately covered waste receptacles need to be provided and made conveniently available for the dog owners to encourage compliance.

Maintain Current Tags and Immunizations

> All dogs must be licensed and current with all required inoculations, and must wear a collar with identification at all times.

All dogs should always be licensed, up to date with required shots, and wearing a collar with identification, whether using a dog park or not! All municipalities try to encourage dog owners to follow through with these requirements, and indicating that they are requirements to use a dog park certainly provides a good incentive. Despite minimal, if any, supervision by authorities, local dog-control officers or police should be encouraged to occasionally spot-check for these items on the dogs in the dog park. That should further promote licensing and the additional requirements.

Leash On Entry and Exit

All dogs must be leashed when entering and exiting [the fenced enclosure]. Leashes must be in the owners' possession at all times.

This rule is about safety. Many dogs are unused to being off leash, and they should be unleashed only within the safe confines of the fenced enclosure. This also relates, of course, to the dog park's design, always providing the transition entry area previously described. That small entrance area fosters the safety aspect of this rule and, indeed, facilitates a safe transition for a dog from being leashed to being unleashed. Thus, on arriving at the dog park, all dogs should be leashed as they approach the entry area. As the owner and dog enter the enclosed transition entrance, the gate they entered should be closed behind them. Next, the owner unleashes their dog and then opens the second gate going into the dog park's large fenced enclosure—there may actually be several transition entries or perhaps several gates off a main transition entrance going into two or more larger fenced enclosures. Often, if there is just one transition entry, there will be an outer entry gate and two interior gates—one for the large-dog area and one for the small-dog area. Having both areas share the entry, each with their own interior entry gate, works well, since only one owner at a time should use the entry space with their dog. When exiting, owners should simply reverse the entry procedure: They should call their dogs, open and go through the interior gate with their dogs, and close the gate behind them. Then, they can securely releash their dogs while in the confines of the small transition enclosure and exit through the outer gate. Again, these procedures provide the safest method possible for both the unleashing of dogs in a dog park and the releasing of dogs following their dog park visit.

Lastly, the latter portion of this rule, concerning leashes being in owners' possession at all times, must also be considered important. Though it may never be necessary for an owner to leash their dog within a fenced enclosure of the dog park, they must always be prepared to do so at a moment's notice. Situations can develop extremely quickly—a dog may become aggressive, an incident may occur between two dogs, or some other occurrence necessitates the leashing and removal of a dog from the dog park, so owners must be prepared accordingly with their leash in hand. Owners should never simply leave their leash on the fence, on a bench, and so on. Unfortunately, I have often seen leashes left in these various places. Even worse, some dog parks offer hooks or even a rack for owners to leave their leashes on!

Supervise and Control

Owners must be inside the dog park, keeping their dogs in view and in voice control at all times.

As much as the social benefit of dog parks is discussed and encouraged for dog owners, their primary responsibility of monitoring their dogs' behavior while

All dog park users are expected to attentively monitor their dogs.

in the dog park's fenced enclosures simply must be prioritized. Owners must realize they are required to supervise their dogs, much as they would supervise their children on a playground. This is related not only to safety, but also to the rule about picking up after your dog. If owners don't actually see their dog defecating, they can't follow that very important rule that truly enables dog parks to work. It also puts the burden on other dog park users to have to point out to you not only the fact that your dog went, but also where. The process can be an awkward and uncomfortable one. The point here is not to put other users in that position. Pay attention to your dog at all times.

The portion of this rule that concerns dogs being in voice control can be difficult for some. Dogs using dog parks should have at least some basic training. One of the basic behavioral skills dogs should be able to exhibit is coming when called by their owner. Ideally, all dogs should be able to respond to their owners' voice accordingly (i.e., they should be in voice control at all times).

Leaving dogs unattended is prohibited.

Dog owners must always be in the fenced enclosure with their dogs. They should never leave their dog in the fenced enclosure for any period of time, even for a minute, even to just get something from the car, even if they intend to come right back, and so on. Owners must simply remain in the dog park with their dogs for the duration of the time they have their dogs in the dog park's fenced enclosure. They must not leave their dogs for any reason. Doing so puts other owners and dogs at risk, including their own dogs, and, again, may put owners in an awkward or even dangerous position. I have even heard of a dog panicking when seeing their owner leave the fenced enclosure, resulting in the only occurrence I have ever heard of a dog scaling a dog park fence.

Prohibitions

Puppies less than 4 months old are prohibited.

The primary reason for this rule, which relates again to safety, is because most puppies have not had all their needed inoculations until they are at least 4 months old. Therefore, they may be susceptible to an assortment of health problems if permitted to be around other dogs, such as in a dog park.

Dogs who are ill, injured, or in heat are prohibited.

This rule essentially relates to common sense. A dog who is ill may, of course, subject other dogs to illness, and may not behave normally. The dog may be uncomfortable or may be taking medication that may alter their behavior. Injuries may be aggravated, especially during active play. Females in heat should never be permitted in a dog park, since males' behavior would be understandably affected, and the likelihood of related problems greatly increases. Again, safety is the operative concern.

Aggressive dogs are not permitted—Owners must remove their dogs on the first sign of aggression toward other dogs or people.

For the benefit of all who use a dog park, aggressive behavior simply cannot be tolerated. This rule is for everyone's safety. No one wants to deal with an aggressive dog, or even take the chance that an aggressive dog may be in a dog park. The fact is that not every dog should be allowed in a dog park—some dogs are simply inappropriate for dog park use, and thus cannot be permitted to do so. Aggressive dogs have no place in a dog park. This, for some, may be an unpopular rule, but again, it is all about safety—for everyone, dogs and people alike.

Dogs must be discouraged from excessive or constant barking—Owners must control or remove their dogs.

Though, as discussed earlier, this is not a common problem, one barker can be disruptive in several ways. It can be problematic to neighbors within earshot of the dog park. I've seen this cause great distress to an entire neighborhood (though there can be simple solutions). Ongoing or frequent barking can be annoying to dog park users, both human and other dogs. Thus, this negatively affects the quality of the dog park experience for all. In addition, one barking dog may start an escalating chain reaction of barking dogs, causing a disturbing, frustrating, and uncomfortable dog park visit instead of a pleasant one. Another concern can be barking that may seem to have aggressive intent. Please note that this rule is not about dogs barking in general; the focus here is excessive or constant barking, which must be considered unacceptable. Occasional barks or yips of joy in a dog park should be considered reasonable and acceptable. For the benefit of all, users should be able to tell the difference. Years ago, during a heated discussion about this rule, I remember a dog park committee member pointing out, very simplistically, "Dogs bark." If an owner is unsure about the amount of their dog's barking, they can try to discourage it or determine the other owners' comfort level. If, however, frequent or ongoing barking cannot be minimized or it appears aggressive, or if the park is in a residential area, it's

Digging should be discouraged, since holes are unsightly and present a hazard to all park users.

better to err on the side of caution. The owner should remove their dog from the facility. For the benefit of all, users should be able to tell the difference.

Dogs must be discouraged from digging—Owners must fill any holes their dogs dig.

Just as some dogs may be barkers, some may be diggers. This problem can be both a hazard and simply unsightly. Holes left by dogs can also become quite messy with rainy weather, enlarging and becoming puddles. The problem may also affect other dog park users in relation to the mud, as well as damage the aesthetics of the dog park. Some dog parks actually leave shovels available for owners who have diggers.

Consuming food and beverages, smoking, and picnicking are prohibited.

This rule is more important than many users realize. When dogs see folks eating or drinking, they are usually interested—some more so than others. It can lead to aggressiveness and conflicts, as well as other behavioral problems. As mentioned earlier, picnic tables should never be placed in or even around a dog park, since it encourages food and beverage consumption. Those bringing dogs to a dog park should be focused on supervising and monitoring their dogs. In addition, eating or drinking can not only shift attention, but also encourage littering and other problematic issues that should not be a part of the dog park experience. In relation to smoking, most smokers tend to put their cigarettes out by stepping on them on the ground. Cigarettes on the ground often interest dogs, who may interpret them as edible. Dogs could also get burned by a cigarette that was simply thrown to the ground or not completely put out when discarded by the smoker. In addition, even items such as food wrappers can be a problem, since dogs may attempt to lick or even eat them. Thus, food and beverages of any type, as well as tobacco products, have no place in a dog park.

Be sure to see the dog park etiquette section later in this chapter.

Optional Rules

The previous rules are basic ones that should apply to all dog parks. The following rules, however, may offer communities some flexibility, which is explained. Unfortunately, there may often be arguments about the establishment of the details of some of these rules; thus, compromise may be required.

It's important to point out that when a dog park is first established, especially as the first dog park in a community, reviewing the initial rules after a period of time (say 6 months or a year) is usually a good exercise. There's no reason that the rules can't be altered or additional ones incorporated.

Limiting the Number of Dogs

The number of dogs is limited to three dogs per person per visit.

This rule is usually to discourage dog walkers, those who are paid to walk dogs, usually several at a time. In addition, of course, how many dogs can be appropriately monitored by one person? Since dog parks always require supervision by users, it may be somewhat challenging for anyone to bring multiple dogs to a dog park. Thus, perhaps a maximum of two dogs may be preferred. Sometimes, a community decides four may be doable. I've seen at least one case where the community considered a five-dog limit because a well-connected, political contributor to their developing dog park had five dogs.

Limiting Participation of Children

Children age 12 and under must be supervised.

There are many options with this rule, and usually no shortage of opinions. In a community considering a rule in relation to children in the dog park, some feel any age should be allowed, while others feel there shouldn't be *any* children allowed in a dog park! The fact is that some determination should be made about children in a dog park because, unfortunately, some children may simply not be safe in a dog park, and their youthful behaviors may put them (or others) at risk. Some concerns include the following:

- Some children, particularly younger ones, can easily be knocked down or run over by larger, exuberant, rambunctious dogs who are just being playful (after all, it is their park).
- Parents or owners can realistically focus on either their child *or* their dog, not both, especially if they bring more than one dog or one child to the dog park.
- Children often run around, shout, scream, or even chase dogs in a dog park, delighted with the many different dogs in the fenced enclosure.

However, those behaviors can often be confusing to the dogs, and thus possibly cause an assortment of problems, from the child's dog feeling he needs to protect the child and becoming territorial over the child to aggressiveness by dogs feeling threatened by a youngster's behavior or noise.

- Finally, dogs can act unpredictably with children. Some who are not familiar with children may chase them or attempt to treat them like their canine playmates, which can lead to a dangerous situation. Sometimes, a child's small size and quick movements may trigger a dog's prey instincts. They may exhibit behaviors such as natural herding tendencies with children.

Thus, the realm of the dangers of small children in dog parks must be viewed seriously by communities, since they determine related rules.

Finally, there's also the issue of deciding on a minimal age for a child to bring a dog to the dog park alone, without a parent or other adult. A community should address these concerns about children in a dog park and enforce them accordingly. The preceding rule, "Children age 12 and under must be supervised," implies that 13-year-olds could bring their dogs to the dog park without a parent or other adult, while 10-year-olds would need a parent or other adult with them in the dog park. It further implies that even toddlers can be in the dog park, as long as an adult is with them. This rule, or any variation thereof, tends to be a controversial one, and it may indeed need to be hashed out.

Small children can get into a lot of trouble in a hurry at a dog park, especially when supervised by adults who are also trying to supervise their dogs.

Off-Leash Requirement

Dogs must be off leash when in the fenced enclosures.

This may be confusing or controversial, especially for new dog park users or dogs that are new to dog parks. The reasoning here is that when dogs are leashed in an atmosphere of unleashed dogs, they may feel vulnerable, defensive, nervous, tense, or generally uncomfortable around the other dogs. A leashed dog in the midst of unleashed dogs is at a disadvantage and cannot display their natural greeting behaviors and body language. They may feel trapped and unable to get away from an unfamiliar dog who approaches too quickly, or they may feel protective toward their owner in relation to an unfamiliar dog. Thus, negative behaviors and even aggression may result, in direct contrast to the positive, enjoyable experience dog parks are supposed to promote and foster. An unleashed dog, even one new to the dog park, who is free to move about can more naturally meet and greet other dogs. Even when introducing a dog to a dog park, it is better to allow the dog the freedom to explore off leash, but owners should stay close, at least at first, for the dog's comfort and safety.

Toys

Be cautious with dog toys; some don't like to share.

Some dog park rules simply prohibit dog toys. There are indeed issues with dog toys in a dog park, but there are also reasons to allow them. Toys can cause possession-related problems that, in turn, can lead to conflicts, aggression, or even fights when dogs attempt to protect their toys. On the other hand, it can be great fun and exercise for dogs to play together with a ball or Frisbee. The allowing, or disallowing, of dog toys in a dog park may come down to owner behavior and common sense. Another concern relating to toys—especially old, ragged, and dirty ones—is when they are left in the dog park as trash or litter; this is always an unpleasant problem.

Other Animals

No animals other than dogs may be brought into the dog park.

Although it seems like a given that dog parks are only for dogs, this rule is more prevalent than some might think. It certainly makes it clear that other types of pets and animals are not only not welcome, but are prohibited from the park. Of course, common sense would dictate that an assortment of problems could result if any other type of animal were brought into the dog park. Thus, including this rule might eliminate the probability that someone might want to bring another type of pet (Cat? Bunny? Ferret?) into the dog park.

Collars

Pinch, choker, pronged, or spiked collars are not permitted—Owners must remove these before taking their dogs into the park.

Prong collars such as this should be prohibited within the dog park, since they present a hazard to playing dogs.

These types of collars are often considered dangerous to dogs—both to the dogs wearing them and to other dogs who may be playing with collar wearers. Dogs' jaws or teeth can get caught on these collars, which can injure or even choke a dog. Owners can remove them in the transition area before entering the fenced enclosure and then place them back on the dog, again in the transition area, when exiting. Ideally these owners should have a regular collar on hand with the appropriate, required tags for their dog to wear in a dog park. This collar should also have a way for the dog to be leashed quickly. This procedure will provide both a safe way for removing and replacing these types of collars and a safe experience for the dogs in the dog park.

Spayed and Neutered Dogs

Only spayed or neutered dogs are allowed.

As an alternative to the rule disallowing dogs in heat, this is a stricter type of constraint. Some, however, feel quite strongly that this is a safer alternative to reducing the opportunity for aggressive behaviors and fights. Certainly, it can encourage dog owners who want to use the dog park to get their dogs spayed or neutered, a concept that always needs to be promoted. However, some may also strenuously object, feeling this rule is simply unfair. Thus, communities will need to decide if they want to establish this rule. The basic version, however (prohibiting dogs in heat from using the dog park), should be considered a minimum standard.

Owner Etiquette

Unfortunately, dog parks are not always filled with responsible owners. As one might then expect, a few unmannerly people can ruin an otherwise pleasant experience for others. That said, all human dog park users should exhibit certain behaviors in order to maximize the many wonderful benefits a community dog park offers. The following information can assist users in enhancing the dog park experience for everyone. These informational items, often referred to as dog park etiquette, should be incorporated in any literature or online material produced in relation to a community's dog park educational programs, especially when a dog park is being developed in a community for the first time.

Follow the Rules

First, and most important, is abiding by the dog park's posted rules. This, of course, helps keep the dog park open and operating as it must in order for it to work. It will also contribute to the positive experience the dogs and their owners can expect to have, as well as keeping the facility safe and preventing incidents and accidents. Beyond the rules, following common courtesies and procedures can help make the dog park truly enjoyable for all.

Know Your Dog

Dog park users must take the time to become an informed owner. They must take their dog's temperament into consideration and must not simply assume their dog is enjoying the dog park or is even a good fit for dog park usage. While most dogs do enjoy dog parks, owners must watch their dog's demeanor and make a judgment call as to how happy the dog is to be there. Some dogs will have no desire to play, yet will enjoy sniffing all the bushes and trees. They may need some time in order to feel truly comfortable. Other dogs will adapt quickly, jumping into the action, meeting and greeting, and will gladly race

Perhaps paying attention and interacting with one's dog is the best way to practice dog park etiquette.

another dog around the park. Other dogs will need more time to adjust, while others still may never seem fit in. Nearly all types of dogs can benefit from the dog park—they just enjoy it in different ways.

For first timers to a dog park, a number of recommendations can help:

- Your very first trip to a dog park should be without your dog to familiarize yourself with the park, how it works, and the posted rules and related information.

- It's best to come at an off-peak time when the park is less busy or crowded—weekday evenings, weekends, and holidays are the busiest times. This is particularly important if your dog has not regularly interacted with other dogs.

- Realize that very typically, as you enter the fenced enclosure from the transitional entry area, many dogs will come over to greet your dog, the new arrival. It's a good idea to encourage your dog to quickly move away from that area, since your dog can easily be overwhelmed by all the attention from unfamiliar dogs, and may even feel cornered or threatened.

- Keep a first visit short to minimize stress and, hopefully, maximize the enjoyment of the new experience.

- Stick close to your dog as they explore during that first dog park experience—dogs may not know what they're expected to do, since this is a new experience in an unfamiliar location. By giving them freedom, but staying close by for safety and comfort, you give dogs a better chance for a positive experience. They usually get it by the second visit. Again, some dogs take longer to adapt, while others do so immediately. Don't be overprotective, but don't be negligent either—your dog will communicate their emotions to you.

Avoid Bringing Children

Although there are usually rules about children in dog parks, it is generally a better idea to simply *not* take children, especially very young ones, into a dog park. Accident possibilities are endless. Children can easily be injured by a romping, well-meaning dog. Many dogs don't know how to behave around small children. Even if your child is wonderful with *your* dog, that doesn't mean their behavior will be appropriate with a strange dog (or vice versa). Again, too, remember that a parent or guardian cannot effectively monitor both a dog and a young child at the same time.

Remedy Behaviors Before Going To a Dog Park

If your dog is aggressive or timid, it's best to remedy these behaviors before bringing them to a dog park. As a general rule, well-behaved, well-socialized dogs do best at a dog park. However, a dog park can be an excellent place to socialize a dog—as long as you stick with them at first, keep them under control, and comfort and encourage them. In addition, as stated previously, try to take your dog to the dog park at less crowded times to allow both of you to acquaint yourselves with the environment without the stress and distraction of multiple

Happy dogs truly enjoy their dog park visits—they socialize, interact, play, run, explore, and get lots of exercise!

dogs. This can also make it easier for your dog to get used to a dog park and learn to behave courteously and nonaggressively.

Pay Attention to Your Pet

Dog owners must always know where their dog is in the dog park and what they are doing. Some inconsiderate owners just let their dog off leash and then proceed to ignore them completely. While chatting and socializing with other dog owners in a dog park is pleasant and considered one of the benefits of community off-leash facilities, monitoring your dog's activities must be done simultaneously. Ignoring your dog, reading the paper or a book, and otherwise not paying attention to your dog can lead to unsafe conditions, attacks, annoyances of people or other dogs, missed feces, accidents, escapes, injuries, and so on. These incidents should not occur, but negligent owners who are not supervising their dogs allow and foster these types of incidents. Thus, owners must always be aware of their dogs' location and their behavior, and they must be able to pick up their dog's feces as quickly as possible. That constant monitoring also may provide the owner with an opportunity to quickly intervene and diffuse a negative situation that might develop.

Any dog with a dominant personality should be particularly closely supervised for any behavior that appears to target less dominant dogs. Also, owners should watch their dog's body language, as well as the body language of the dogs their dog is interacting with, and should be prepared to interrupt inappropriate play on the part of any dog. In addition, no one likes an owner who pretends not to notice when their dog relieves itself or when their dog is repeatedly humping another. Lastly, it is recommended that you stay connected to your dog by calling them back occasionally for a pat on the head or a hug, then letting them resume play with their canine pals.

Don't Discipline Someone Else's Dog

If you must use some force to separate dogs, so be it, but never attempt to punish someone else's dog once the conflict has ended. If you find another dog's behavior unacceptable, and the owner doesn't do anything about it, take your dog out of the dog park rather than attempting to correct someone else's dog. Don't pick up or grab someone else's dog without permission—you might get bitten, inadvertently injure a dog, or find yourself in an uncomfortable confrontation with the dog's owner.

Respect Differences

Dogs play in many different ways in a dog park. Some dogs like to play chase, others may enjoy rough and tumble play, and still others may be more interested in games with people, such as Frisbee catching. Be aware that each canine has their own levels of dominance or submissiveness that affect the way they play with other dogs. This is why supervision is so important. For example, if your dog's favorite activity becomes persistent humping, this behavior must be discouraged; more often than not, the dog being humped will eventually become angry. Often too, this situation will upset the owner of the dog being humped. Again, owners must always monitor their dog's behavior in a dog park.

If your dog is playing rather vigorously with another dog and that dog or their owner seem uncomfortable with it, you should attempt to refocus your dog elsewhere. Even when playing, it is not uncommon for larger or heavier dogs to roughhouse a bit too much and intimidate younger or smaller dogs. If necessary, ask the other owner if they're comfortable with the way your dog is playing with their dog. Some folks may be uncomfortable with the way dogs may establish a hierarchy in a dog park, yet may not speak up. Obviously, since everyone wants to have a positive, enjoyable experience at the dog park, respecting one another's comfort level plays an important role—for both people and dogs.

Don't Overdress

Though it's not polite for dogs to jump on people, it's also impolite and inappropriate to become terribly upset if a dog in a dog park enthusiastically jumps up, getting dirt or mud on you. It is, after all, a dog park. Owners need to realize that dirt and mud should be considered a part of the dog park scene, and they should dress down accordingly for that aspect of the experience.

Be Cautious About Advice

Be careful about taking advice from other dog park users who are not canine professionals. Most dog park users truly mean well and like to help others if they feel they can. However, their helpful ideas are often simply based on their own personal experiences, not on proven, professional information or techniques.

Thus, caution should be used whenever advice is offered or given. One's own veterinarian should be the first resource sought for both health and behavioral concerns.

Remove Your Dog When Necessary

Most of the reasons for needing to do this have been identified, but this section puts most of the reasons in one place.

- Certainly, if your dog shows signs of aggression, unprovoked snarling, growling, or any attack displays, you must remove them immediately.
- If your dog exhibits constant, nonstop barking, you should remove them from the park.
- If your dog is intimidating or annoying other dogs or being a bully, and you can't effectively stop them from doing so, you should remove your dog. This will essentially be a courtesy to others, and it may save you the frustration of having your dog viewed as aggressive, especially when the behavior is actually a reaction to a specific situation or other dog.
- Since fights or other negative occurrences can erupt when dogs are over-stimulated or overtired, learn to recognize the signs that your dog has had enough play time in the dog park, and take them home.
- If a person or dog enters the dog park who makes you feel uncomfortable or nervous, leave and plan to return at another time.

This dog is tired and trying to rest. Monitoring one's dog means recognizing when your dog may be ready to go home.

Basically, everyone should use common sense and their best judgment to determine when it is time to remove their dog from the dog park.

Dealing With Conflicts

If someone complains about your dog's behavior, be prepared to consider their perspective before becoming defensive. Apologize if your dog has been inappropriate. If necessary, you should be willing to take your dog and leave if you can't control the behavior. Meanwhile, it's always important to be polite and reasonable, even if other users are problematic. Certainly, if someone else's dog is behaving inappropriately or if a user isn't following the rules and isn't controlling their dog, speak up. Perhaps assume they don't know any better or they haven't read the rules. You can introduce yourself and gently and politely educate them or remind them of a rule, and thank them when they comply. If you're uncomfortable about doing this, perhaps seek out the support of another park user. As a responsible dog park user, you have an obligation to report inappropriate actions of other users that put the safety of dogs and people at risk. This also applies to the general operation of the dog park and the related issues and concerns that could threaten the safe, smooth functioning of the park.

Some examples of positive phrases:

- "Excuse me, but perhaps you didn't realize that this portion of the dog park is for dogs under 30 pounds (14 kg). Your lab is really handsome; I bet he'd love to play with the golden retriever in the large-dog area."

- "That sandwich sure looks tasty! It looks like there's a Saint Bernard headed this way eyeing it! It might be safer to finish it outside the fence and then bring your dog back in to play."

- "What a cute baby you have! If she were mine, I'd be a bit worried about having her here in the dog park with all these energetic dogs running around."

If the inappropriate actions of others are putting you or your dog at risk in any way, and the other dog owner isn't receptive to your suggestions or reminders, take your dog and leave the park under the heading of better safe than sorry. Then you can contact the park authorities about the situation. If you couldn't obtain the user's name and contact information, you can try to get their license plate number. If that's not possible, you can write down a detailed description of both the person and the dog, noting any times you've seen them at the dog park to help authorities to make contact. In addition, write a detailed but unemotional description of the behavior or incident that you felt was inappropriate. Generally, though, a positive approach works better with people, just as it does with dogs.

Following these etiquette tips, along with the dog park rules, can truly maximize and enhance the enjoyment for all. Dog parks involve self-policing, and thus self-enforcement. These concepts make dog parks work, but they involve responsible, polite, caring, positive folks with a common-sense attitude. This enables a dog park to operate successfully and assures wonderful dog park experiences for everyone!

Communicating Guidelines Through Signage

It's important to ensure that certain basic information concerning park use (not just the rules) is made readily available to users. Thus, the following should be incorporated on the dog park signage:

- A statement indicating that owners must realize they are legally responsible for their dogs and injuries caused by them to other dogs or people. This is usually the case under most circumstances anywhere.

  As discussed earlier, when a municipality creates a dog park facility as a benefit for its community and provides the proper signage indicating that users are welcome to bring their dogs into the enclosure where they will encounter dogs off leash, it is difficult to make a successful claim against the local government if a dog or person is injured. However, if an irresponsible owner does not control their dog properly, they may very well be liable for their behavior and they must be aware of this fact on entering a dog park. Some dogs should simply not use a dog park, and owners need to realize whether their dogs are good candidates, based on their dog's temperament, demeanor, behavior, and so on. In other words, if their dog has exhibited inappropriate behavior or aggressiveness when around other dogs (or people) in the past, perhaps they should reconsider taking their dogs to a dog park. An injury or similar incident can certainly be tragic, but it can also be costly if a lawsuit results from the incident.

- A notice that failure to abide by the dog park rules may result in loss of dog park privileges, removal from the dog park, or fines

- Hours should be listed, such as "The dog park is open from sunset to dusk," 7:00 a.m. to 7:00 p.m., 6:00 a.m. to 8:00 p.m., and so on.

- Emergency information and telephone numbers (local police, animal control, parks and recreation department). In a dog park, an emergency could be an injury (dog or person), an argument, or a fight (dog or people). Thus, the availability of emergency phone numbers on the signage is important. It's the same sort of info that would be on any park signage.

- The name, location, and telephone numbers of the agency responsible for the dog park

- Information about how to register complaints

- The municipality or agency's hold harmless clause. This is essentially a provision that states that users agree to not hold the sponsoring agency responsible for any loss, damage, or legal responsibility. The users agree to assume all legal liability and responsibility, relieving the agency of any liability; thus, the dog park users (i.e., the dog owners) must accept this responsibility in relation to their use of the dog park. This is a common legal provision for most, if not all, government entities.

- An explanation about entering the fenced enclosures through the transition entry areas, including the differences between the different fenced enclosures (i.e., the small-dog area is for dogs 30 pounds and under, while the large dog area is for dogs over 30 pounds)

- Information indicating that the dog park may periodically close temporarily for routine maintenance, special programs or events, or emergencies

For a dog park to be everything a community envisions, rules must be followed, common courtesies must be extended, and common sense must be applied. This chapter reflects the operating system of a dog park, the how-to manual that lists the procedures that make a dog park run successfully—by its users! Dog parks are wonderful facilities for both dogs and people when the rules of safety and courtesy are followed by all!

The next chapter is about the *big* day—the grand opening of the dog park! When they say every dog has its day, *this*, then, is that day!

7

The Grand Opening

A grand dog park deserves a grand opening! Find out how to celebrate your new park's introduction in style.

The big day has finally arrived! Dog owners are excited! All the hard work has come to fruition, and the entire community is ready!

Chances are, if this is a first dog park in a community, part of the excitement will involve basic curiosity. Many folks may not have ever seen, or been in, or even heard of a dog park. Some may have heard about dog parks, but have never actually experienced one. They will be in for quite a treat, as will everyone else who comes to the grand opening!

This chapter is an overview of how to make this wonderful, much-looked-forward-to event truly an exciting, fun day for all. Even if your dog park begins with a soft opening, which this chapter explains, the grand-opening festivities should make for a terrific community happening!

Planning, Preparing, and Publicizing

The planning group should select a target opening date well in advance. In most cases, as with any special event, several months of planning will probably be needed. As development progresses, getting everything in place in the dog park for opening day should be a priority. I can't emphasize enough avoiding excuses like "We'll just have to open without the benches," or "We'll put the fountain in later on." Opening the dog park should provide the community with what has been expected and anticipated all along—a complete, new facility with all the basic required amenities, as the publicity promised. Certainly, other features, such as a play piece or sculpture, may be added to the dog park later on. More amenities, such as more benches, another water fountain, or perhaps an additional shade structure may enhance an already established dog park. However, for opening day, the park should look and be complete! Thus, *everything* should be ready.

A committee or subcommittee, an individual volunteer, or group of people may be responsible for planning the opening day. They can determine, as for any special event, the who, what, where, when, and how of the day. Thus, they should decide who will be invited to attend and who will lead, conduct, and participate in the festivities; what the activities and features of the day will include; where, *exactly*, each of the components of the day will take place; what the schedule of the day's events will involve; and finally, how the day will play out.

Publicity efforts should begin when the dog park is conceived and should continue throughout the planning process. Even if there have been ups and downs, challenges, and bad news along the way, the local media should be included from day one. Frankly, in most cases (as mentioned in an earlier chapter), the naysayers, even if there are only a few, are a common mainstay of the dog park process more often than not. Seldom does everything go completely smoothly. However, the problems will be dealt with, hashed out, and, eventually resolved, one way or another. Thus, the off-leash facility will move forward. That said, opening day will be eagerly anticipated with great enthusiasm from all factions of the community.

Regular publicity about the progress of the dog park's development helps build that positive attitude and excitement. Ideally, with photographs as well as regular news reports and stories, the anticipation will build as the park's grand

Local media will appreciate the opportunity to cover the grand opening.

opening day approaches. Thus, the media should be strongly encouraged and should be let in on the plans for the event. Several articles, photos, interviews, or other items should be components of the upcoming celebration in local newspapers, radio, and television, as well as advertised online. This means including both local and regional media personalities, putting features on radio and television shows, and, of course, taking advantage of social media (such as Facebook and Twitter) to publicize the upcoming celebration. Hopefully, the dog park supporters and fundraising groups have been keeping their social-media followers informed all along. Thus, lots of interested community members have been looking forward to the opening of the dog park for some time!

Beginning several weeks in advance, a flier, brochure, or announcement should be published and distributed to get the word out about the big day coming soon. Some type of graphic image or logo should have already been developed so the community recognizes and relates to the visual image of the new dog park. That recognition will foster enthusiasm.

In addition, as the opening day gets closer, whether or not indicated on the flier, a schedule of activities should be publicized so the community knows what to expect at the celebration. Make sure, too, that it's clearly indicated that the celebration location is just *outside* of the dog park. This enables, encourages, and exhibits the proper use of the dog park as it opens to the community.

The flier should include lots of simple but important information. For example, indicate *exactly* where the new dog park is located, maybe even including a simple, small map on the flier. The information should also, of course, clearly indicate the starting time and perhaps the specific park area locations for the festivities. Information should also be included as to the necessity for all dogs to be on leash when they come to the festivities. It can then be mentioned that the dogs can, of course, go off leash inside the dog park when it actually opens that day. Make sure the flier includes a phone number or e-mail address for folks to easily contact if they have questions. Other appropriate information on the flier could be sponsors, important community leaders in attendance, entertainment, or any or all of the other planned features listed in this chapter. The idea here is to encourage all community members to come and celebrate this very special, exciting day!

One great feature related to early positive publicity for establishing a dog park is to create a large sign well in advance of opening day and strategically place it where the dog park is to be built, announcing something like "Coming soon! Future home of the Anytown dog park." Additional information on the sign could include a tentative opening date, such as Coming to This Site in Fall 2013 or Coming in March 2014. The sign could have additional information, such as "Contact Jane Doe of the Anytown dog park committee, 123-456-7890 to learn more, donate, or get involved!" Or "Check out the dog park committee's website, www.anytowndogpark.com." Whatever information is placed on the sign, it should generate positive anticipation and excitement for the municipality. It will get community members talking, interested, and, hopefully, involved! In addition, it can be erected early on, as soon as the site becomes *official*.

Features and Festivities

Communities can certainly choose from lots of different features to celebrate their dog park's opening. Some are basic, traditional types of celebratory activities, while some are perhaps more unusual. Communities can personalize the components of their grand opening to make the event truly unique. The day should be joyous and fun for all, but especially for the newbies to dog parks. It should be interesting and exciting, a day to remember. Typically, a dog park's grand opening may include the following options.

Information

The grand opening is an ideal opportunity to exchange information with all the community members interested in the dog park! Now is the time to let people know exactly what the dog park is and how to use it. It's also the time to answer questions, clarify any confusion, and make sure people are well informed and prepared to take advantage of the park. Let's consider the ways information can be exchanged at the opening event:

- The media must be in attendance. They will be happy to be there for a good-news event and celebration. Reporters and other various media professionals should be sure to bring along photographers, since there will be terrific photo ops at a dog park opening!
- A number of handouts may be distributed at the event. These can help those new to dog parks understand how they work, why they work, and what wonderful facilities they are in a community. Examples of handouts to be considered include the following:

○ An official program of the celebration, listing the agenda, speakers, committees involved, municipal officials, and so on

○ Rules of the dog park

○ Description of the dog park

○ Map of the dog park

○ Dog park etiquette

○ Benefits of dog parks

○ Description of how to enter and exit the transition entry areas

○ Description of the story of the dog park: how it evolved or came to be

○ Description of how the dog park will be maintained

• Some communities may want folks to register in some fashion. If there are to be usage fees, the grand opening can be the ideal time to encourage sign-ups and have interested patrons pay fees. The municipality may accept payments at a table as they distribute the tags or cards to be used.

• If a community is planning to conduct programs in their new dog park, program registration may also be a feature of the day. It's certainly the perfect opportunity to showcase some coming attractions at the dog park. Whether there will be basic dog obedience classes, agility training, the American Red Cross's pet first aid course, or holiday special events for pets, folks attending the grand opening of the dog park will most likely be very receptive to and interested in the program opportunities. Make sure that a list is posted or handouts are available describing the upcoming offerings of new programs.

Activities and Entertainment

What's an opening celebration without fun activities and entertainment for all? Your event should reflect the advantages of your particular park, as well

Various community organizations and businesses will want to have their support displayed at the celebration.

as the special needs and interests of your community. Consider some of the many options:

• Several speakers should be scheduled, but they should plan to keep their remarks brief, since there will be dozens, if not far more, dogs and their owners waiting for the *big* moment when they can finally enter the new facility. Speakers may include the mayor or supportive politicians who were instrumental in helping the dog park become a reality, the head of the parks and recreation agency responsible for the new facility, the lead volunteer who spearheaded the quest and worked hard for the dog park, or any appropriate community leader or member who played a role in the park's development—a local veterinarian, a media person, a landscape architect, an important donor or contributor, and so on. Each community will have their own important cast of characters. Again, though, remember that excited attendees will practically be chomping at the bit to do what they came to do—get inside that new dog park to romp and play, meet and greet, and run and explore!

• Have an official ribbon cutting, leash cutting, or even leash *chewing* ceremony. Call it what you will, but this is an important focal point of the festivities.

• Sometimes a dog parade (or dog *and people* parade) is a fun feature of the day. Everyone enjoys this activity—it's a treat for participants and spectators alike and a genuine family affair! Sometimes folks dress up their dogs, or both the dogs and owners dress alike. It's great fun, and absolutely everyone is smiling for this event! Be sure that leashes are used if the parade is not held in a fenced enclosure. Talk about photo ops!

• The grand opening of a dog park is also a wonderful venue for dog-related contests—with prizes, of course! The categories can be numerous and as creative as can be. Some traditional examples include the following:

  ○ Best Dressed
  ○ Most Adorable
  ○ Best Mirror Image (dog and owner look alike)
  ○ Best Pet Trick
  ○ Most Obedient
  ○ Best Vocal Performance (by a dog)
  ○ Best Tail-Wagger
  ○ Biggest
  ○ Smallest

The possibilities are endless. The more imaginative, the better! Everyone enjoys these fun, often silly contests. Whatever the dogs do, rightly or wrongly, the crowd will cheer, laugh, and thoroughly enjoy these contests! Again, they add to the wonderful, festive feeling everyone will have throughout the day.

• A scavenger hunt, a Chalk-It-Up sidewalk art event, or even some raffles or games are additional examples of fun, family-oriented features for a dog park's grand opening. Communities often have their own favorite familiar activities that no celebration should be without.

- Music can certainly be included in the festivities. Whether it's familiar tunes played by a DJ or live music played by local musicians or the high school band, music is a welcome part of any celebration—it adds to the fun and excitement of the day and makes the atmosphere that much more festive.

- Any dog-related entertainment (e.g., agility or Frisbee dog demonstrations) is always a particularly special treat for those in attendance.

- Along with the music mentioned previously, a remote broadcast from a radio station is often a fun feature of a special event like a dog park opening. Local radio stations are often happy to have an opportunity to be a part of a community happening. It offers them publicity and exposure for their sponsors, and people tend to get a kick out of seeing and hearing live radio. Perhaps they could play dog-oriented songs throughout the day—"How Much is That Doggie in the Window?", "Walking the Dog," or "Who Let the Dogs Out?"

- Giveaways for dogs are very common features at the opening of a new dog park. Local pet vendors, pet supply shops, manufacturers of pet products or food, and those offering various types of pet services often offer dog treats, toys, sample food packs, bandanas, or other free items. The giveaways will probably have advertising on them, so it's a win–win for everyone! Plus, these things add to the excitement of the festivities, and who doesn't like freebies?

- Not surprisingly, giveaways for people are also popular at a dog park's grand opening celebration. All sorts of businesses, in addition to the previously mentioned pet-oriented vendors, may be in attendance and may offer all sorts

Silent auctions are a popular fundraising event at grand openings.

of freebies for attendees: pens, water bottles, hats, T-shirts, you name it! Again, it all adds to the festiveness of the day.

- Raffles and auctions might also be a part of the day, often as a fundraiser for the new park.

Exhibits and Vendors

Many organizations will be interested in taking part in the dog park's big day. Their presence not only enhances the festive atmosphere, but also connects them with a captive audience of consumers, so you can be sure they'll be happy to participate!

- As with any celebration, refreshments are always an expected, appreciated feature. Whether the refreshments are free or available for sale, they are a typically considered a staple of a special event. There's plenty of opportunity, too, for food vendors to be creative at a dog park opening by providing dog-themed offerings, such as bone-shaped cookies or perhaps a special deal for the day on their hot *dogs*. When making arrangements for food vendors, this creative aspect can be encouraged. It adds to the fun of the day.

- Pet items may be offered by vendors who bring an assortment of their goods to the event for sale. These can include dog collars, toys, food and water bowls, dog beds, treats and chews, or dog-food products. These vendors like the opportunity to take their show on the road, bringing their products to the dog

Vendors will jump at the chance to get a captive audience with dog park users!

Agility dogs love to strut their stuff for an audience, so it's a great idea to invite agility groups to the grand opening celebration.

owners rather than the dog owners coming to them! Vendors who attend may also sell miscellaneous items that may or may not relate to dogs, but they appreciate the opportunity to be a part of the community celebration. Though these types of vendors may seem a bit unusual, some communities may encourage their attendance, since some may be dog lovers, some may have been popular supporters of the dog park, and some may have been involved with the dog park committee. Some communities may simply invite and encourage all local businesses to be involved in the celebration!

• Local shelters and rescue organizations are often featured at dog park openings with a table or booth, and they may even bring along dogs available for adoption. They bring literature, highlight their services with exhibits, and usually accept much-needed donations at the event. Due to the festive mood, the celebration usually brings much goodwill to these agencies and groups.

• Local veterinarians and other pet professionals may want to attend and have the opportunity to meet and greet attendees and their dogs. They may also bring literature about their services.

• Often, educational demonstrations are a feature of a dog park's grand opening—K9 units with local police, assistance dogs or therapy dogs, and dogs from agility groups all like to show what they can do. Most folks really enjoy seeing and learning about dogs involved in these various types of work and

Dog-related services, often offered as additional fundraising opportunities, are appreciated and used at a dog park opening. This oversized pup is about to get a bath in an undersized pool!

activities, especially those who help people. For most people, it's a rare opportunity, and it is educational for all.

• Sometimes, services such as nail clipping, dog baths, or microchipping may be offered at the event. These can be used as fundraisers. Attendees are often pleased to take advantage of the offerings and are happy to know their fees (or a portion thereof) support the new dog park.

So, with the preceding information as an overview of many examples of the features of a grand opening of a dog park, picking and choosing activities should be easy. However, just as with any parks event, the parks department or sponsoring agency should have their professionals involved from day one. They'll be the ones who will make sure all the needed basics are included to ensure a safe, smoothly running event for all involved. They'll bring first aid kits, they'll make sure restroom facilities are clean, ready, and appropriately equipped, and they'll make sure the police and emergency service professionals are either on hand or are at least alerted that crowds will be at the park that day. They'll plan to have staff overseeing the event to help out as needed, answer questions, and have extra equipment available (an extension cord, for example). They'll make sure plenty of garbage cans are available, especially near where food is being sold and consumed. In other words, these are the folks who keep the event running smoothly and think of all the things that others may often forget. They simply must be involved to ensure the success of the event, above and beyond the planned featured highlights of the celebration.

Soft Opening

Often, a dog park may actually open to the public, usually without publicity, before the grand opening date. This may be done for any number of reasons. The park may be finished and ready ahead of schedule. People will be eager to try it out, even though the grand opening is set for several weeks (or even months) later. Sometimes a soft opening enables a trial run for rules, especially if some of them were originally controversial. Temporary signage can be posted in case some of the rules change or other information proves to be desirable before the more expensive, permanent signs for the park are ordered. A soft opening can also be viewed as a dry run; this is particularly helpful if kinks need to be worked out before the grand opening date. A bench, because it's in direct sun, may need to be moved

Using temporary signage for a soft opening allows for changes to be made when the permanent signage is created. This can be especially helpful with dog park rules that require more testing for community approval.

to a different area of the dog park, surfacing issues may come up that need to be addressed, the hours may need to be altered, or parking issues may arise. Whatever the situation, a soft opening can alleviate unexpected problems at the dog park before the official grand opening, thus enabling an even more successful celebration!

So, as we head off to the next chapter about evaluating the new facility, we need to ask ourselves, "How'd we do?" Is our dog park the cat's meow or, instead, are we in the doghouse? Fact is, we must evaluate our creation. It's easy, once it's up and running, to treat it like, say, a basketball court—what's there to do? Or, perhaps treat it like a picnic area, just removing the garbage on schedule. A dog park, especially throughout the first year of operation, needs to be monitored. It would be unrealistic to assume all will go perfectly from day one. That would be terrific, but it's simply unlikely. Monitoring will allow issues or problems to be recognized and dealt with, quickly and efficiently. Thus, evaluating the new dog park is an important step to ensure that the dog park is operating properly, that users are following the rules, that the facility is being maintained as it should, and so on. Unexpected problems are not uncommon, but they must be recognized as such so they can be addressed and solved as soon as possible.

Now let's determine if our new dog park has really gone to the dogs…

Evaluation: Concerns, Problems, and Solutions for Success

The new dog park is up and running! How's it going? Ongoing evaluation is an important part of making sure the dog park remains valuable to the community.

Evaluation is always important in recreation and parks. Though we usually think about evaluating programs, events, and staff, a new facility should be evaluated as well, especially if it's the first dog park in a community. This chapter identifies and explores the various topics that should be evaluated and discusses examples of common problems and concerns—all with an eye toward a successful, well-operated, well-maintained dog park facility.

The evaluation should be conducted by the department or agency responsible for the new facility. Ideally, that should be a professional recreation and parks administrator or supervisor. Volunteers, no matter how sincere, dedicated, and involved they have been throughout the project process, cannot have the understanding or experience that a professional brings. However, volunteers can certainly assist a professional in conducting an evaluation. Their ongoing passion and interest may prove to be valuable assets. Ideally, professionals will be objective and will focus their approach on the long-term success of the facility.

We begin by reflecting on the original recommended components, as identified in chapter 4. Let's review each of the categories and topics.

Design Elements

These items relate to the layout, the natural features, and the structural elements of the dog park. Since these can be identified as the basic aspects of the facility, any evaluation should begin with them.

Design and Layout

The design of the facility, including the fashion in which it has been laid out, should be functioning well, as it was planned and envisioned. Perhaps there

Notice how a dog along the fencing to the right would not be visible from the bench due to a sight line problem—and this is a small dog enclosure!

have been some problem places within or even outside of the fencing. Locations where problems are occurring could relate, for example, to specific design features, perimeter concerns, or ground conditions.

Any visual concerns, such as sight lines or feature placement, should also be identified, especially since those concerns relate to the users' ability to monitor their dogs. Ideally, of course, if the dog park's design was created with sound principles in mind (e.g., making the two primary enclosures large enough, avoiding right angles, and creating the transition area correctly), it is unlikely that design problems will be discovered in an evaluation.

Unexpected problems, however, may arise due to unanticipated circumstances. For the most part, the following are all quite common effects of overcrowding in park use in general, but here, we see the nuances of this in the context of a dog park. One example here, which is not uncommon, relates to greater than expected usage. Though the size of one or both of the fenced enclosures may be adequate by the minimum standard recommendation of the enclosures totaling at least one acre, usage may prove to dictate a larger amount of property is needed. The original size of the design is thus inadequate. Indications of this can be numerous. Surfacing, regardless of the type, suffers with overuse. There may be issues with large numbers of dogs at typical high usage times, as well as conflicts with owners.

Acceptable solutions to the problems encountered should be determined and carried out, though cost must be considered with unanticipated problems. In the example concerning the popularity of the facility and resulting overuse ramifications, that could mean enlarging the facility (if additional property is available), relocating the facility, creating an additional dog park in the community, or somehow solving the problem administratively (controlling the usage). The concern, however challenging, must be viewed seriously and addressed. Be sure to recognize that many park professionals would classify this as a good problem; whenever lots of people want to take advantage of a parks program, event, or facility to the point that the park has more users than expected, they may conclude that they've done their jobs well.

Other design problems tend to be quite site specific, and may often be very different from one dog park to another. The problems may relate to terrain, climate, or weather, proximity to other park features, or even the interests of the users. Plus, since the design and layout of a dog park relate to the available property and the site, shape, and topography of the land (versus standard measurements as for various sports fields), the opportunity for unanticipated design-related issues is vast. Again though, following the recommendations for proven best practices, as indicated throughout this book, will usually prevent or minimize problems.

Natural Features and Elements

The natural aspects and features of a dog park create a uniqueness and character that each community can proudly call its own. These elements in the space used for the dog park may be very attractive and may provide interest for both the dogs and their owners to enjoy and perhaps explore. On the other hand, these same elements may present problems for the users. Perhaps problems will not

The wear and tear on the surfacing in a dog park can be problematic aesthetically. More importantly, it can pose a safety concern. Surfacing issues must be addressed in a timely manner or they will simply get worse.

emerge when the dog park first opens, but, as we all know, things happen. Trees and shrubs continue to grow and need to be maintained, a tree can be struck by lightning or damaged by severe weather, thereby creating a hazard, and various types of terrain and natural features, such as rock outcroppings or a sloped area, may exhibit erosion or runoff problems, especially following rainy weather. Another concern here would have to be in relation to the natural shade areas (versus shade structures) in the dog park. Perhaps the amount and location of the natural shade has proven to be inadequate. Users may complain about too much or too little shade. Shade, or the lack thereof, can cause or relate to other types of problems, such as surfacing deterioration. All these issues may arise when evaluating the natural elements of a dog park.

Often, we don't expect or anticipate the natural features in and near our park facilities to create usage issues. We may simply believe they are just there—they will always be there and they need nothing from us. Ideally, the natural elements are attractive and enhance the experience of park users in various ways. The fact is, however, that those features must be cared for from time to time to assess their condition, to maintain them appropriately, and to prevent problems from occurring.

Structural Elements

These elements, added to the park space or property, essentially delineate the dog park facility. These items primarily include the fencing, gates, and the hardscape and landscape areas.

The fencing, if properly selected and professionally installed, including being of the correct height, having top and bottom rails and self-latching gates, and so on, should not be problematic. It should serve well for years with minimal attention needed. If corners were cut, however, fencing problems may indeed occur. For example, if bottom rails were not included, dogs who are diggers may try to dig under a section of fencing; properly installed bottom rails make that digging difficult, and thus far less likely that dogs could actually dig their way out of the enclosure. Though this scenario is quite unlikely, I'll emphasize again the importance of doing your dog park right—top and bottom rails on fencing need to be considered a must-do to create a dog park correctly, professionally, and safely.

The dog park's hardscape areas are important in numerous ways (see chapter 4). They may be made of several different types of materials, and may

Without a bottom rail, the bottom of the fencing is very flexible. With minimal effort, a dog could push their way underneath, or worse, get caught and possibly injured.

create hard surfaces in different ways. In colder climates, heaving problems may be experienced. In some areas within the dog park, roots may grow, eventually disrupting the hardscape. With brick-paved hardscape areas, the importance of correct installation can't be emphasized enough. They may need some periodic maintenance to prevent problems, such as separation and weed growth between them. Keep in mind that any hard surface material may develop puddles, especially if not installed well. Other problems, especially weather-related ones, may occur at the edges of hardscape areas, where the rest of the dog park surfacing (natural grass or others) meets the hard surfaces.

Regardless of the type of problem experienced in relation to the hardscape areas of the dog park, an evaluation should identify them, determine the cause (if not obvious), and indicate the needed correction or solution. Issues of this type should be considered safety hazards (e.g., tripping hazards), and thus should be given priority status when resolving dog park facility concerns. In addition, though not as important, problems with hardscape areas, especially when left unaddressed for a period of time, may be unsightly. They can make an otherwise attractive, welcoming park facility look shabby, unkempt, and ill maintained.

Lastly, hard surfaces may also be in the ancillary locations around the dog park's fenced enclosures. As part of the dog park area and dog park experience, these areas should be evaluated as well. For example, parking areas and walkways should be considered here. If there are additional related spaces, such as restrooms or places for owners to bathe their dogs, these areas should also be reviewed as part of the evaluation.

If left unattended, the weed growth and cracked blocks in these photos will get worse and will eventually become more difficult, and costly, to resolve.

Evaluation reveals that the apron planned for this park is not large enough; it should be expanded.

Equipment

All equipment in any park facility should be maintained to foster long life, adequate usability, and appropriate, aesthetically pleasing attractiveness. This, of course, encourages park usage and community pride. This is certainly true of the various types of equipment present in a dog park.

An evaluation of a dog park should address each of the various types of equipment comprehensively. The primary equipment items include benches, fountains, waste-bag stations, waste cans, and signage. In any given dog park, there may be multiples of each of these items or other items, sometimes simply decorative ones. Each piece should be identified and considered when conducting the evaluation. In fact, it's a good idea to create an inventory of the items while conducting the evaluation, especially if no current inventory list exists. The inventory list may assist the agency in regard to future purchases, problems, maintenance, and so on.

Benches

Since there are literally hundreds of different types of park benches, varying by size, style, design, color, materials, price, quality, and so on, evaluating them may seem challenging. In reality, the evaluation should simply determine whether they are meeting the goals originally set when they were selected and purchased.

First, there should be an adequate number of well-located benches in each of the fenced enclosures. Perhaps the most common problem is simply not having enough benches. Though many users enjoy interacting with their dogs in a dog park, most want to sit down for some period of time during their visit. Thus, an adequate number of benches is very important. This is actually a simple, solvable problem, but its frequency and prevalence is baffling.

With no shade on a sunny day and placed in the middle of the park, making it difficult to watch your dog, this otherwise attractive bench is very poorly located.

Without adequate benches in a dog park, users bring their own residential (versus commercial) seating, and often leave it behind. That creates a poor aesthetic look to the park and, more importantly, a potential liability concern.

Benches that are well located may simply reflect usage. If there are enough benches in the dog park to accommodate the users but they're not being used, they may be located poorly. Perhaps they are too far from the entrance gates or they are undesirably located for other reasons that should be determined and corrected.

The benches in a dog park, as in any park, should be of commercial quality, chosen for their ability to maintain their look, color, and condition for a good number of years. Ideally, they should be vandal and graffiti resistant. The base installation should also be evaluated. It should be in good condition, without, for example, erosion or other problems causing exposed footings.

Finally, determine users' level of satisfaction with the benches. In conducting a dog park evaluation, users are often forthcoming with comments, especially in relation to benches.

Fountains

The fountains in the dog park, of which there are now several types and several manufacturers, need to be installed properly and operating satisfactorily. Though most need minimal attention and are manufactured to deter vandalism, just as with any plumbing fixtures, problems may occur. Ideally, they have been located well in the dog park and they are being used. There should not be rust, corrosion, leaks, puddles, or drainage or usage problems. Any issues with the fountains should be addressed as needed in a timely manner.

Since many fountains in a dog park have separate fixtures for use by both dogs and their owners, all aspects of the fountains should be evaluated. If there is a bib feature, it should be working properly as well.

The exterior condition of the fountains should also be evaluated. As with other equipment elements, the fountain should maintain its condition, color, and look for years of use.

Waste Stations

Since there are now numerous types of waste stations and bags, selection may have been somewhat difficult. However, as long as the units are meeting expectations, are in good working condition, are well located, are being used regularly, as required of all dog owners, and are being regularly replenished, all should be well. One of the most frequent problems encountered with waste-bag stations is with the type that has the bags on a roll, which may enable users to remove far more bags than they actually need in the dog park—it's much like taking toilet paper off the roll. This means refilling may need to be more frequent. Many bags are wasted. Users may attempt to stuff bags back into the station unit, or some may purposely remove extra bags to use elsewhere. (Some consider this stealing.) A number of manufacturers of these waste-bag stations no longer make the type that requires the bags to be on a roll; however, many communities still have and purchase this type. Hopefully, signage may help in this matter.

There are seldom problems with waste cans. As indicated in chapter 4, however, they should be of a type that is covered securely and does not have an open top. Of course, there needs to be enough of them. They should also be easily and regularly emptied, conveniently located (often near a waste-bag station), and, as with all dog park equipment, well maintained. Users should, of course, use the waste cans, especially to dispose of their used waste bags of dog feces. Indeed, when evaluating the dog park, perhaps the most important aspect concerning waste cans is that they are, in fact, being used regularly. If not, reasons and solutions should be determined. If, for example, owners are not picking up after their dogs and, thus, are not using the waste cans as they should, this may actually indicate some other dog park problems. These might

Signage must be kept clean, visible, readable, and in good repair.

relate to waste-bag replenishment, the locations of the waste-bag station or waste cans, or, of course, signage.

Evaluation is certainly important when discussing waste in a dog park. Keeping waste stations replenished with waste bags and making sure waste cans are emptied regularly simply must be considered priorities in dog park operations. These tasks alone, in many cases, can determine the level of success a dog park may experience. If bags are not available, owners may not pick up after their dogs, thus causing users to break what is perhaps the cardinal rule of dog parks—picking up after your dog. If waste cans are not emptied regularly, perhaps leading to overflow, the resulting mess and smell may either drive users away or cause them to simply add to the piled waste around the base of the waste can. Either way, if these are identified as problems, they must be corrected in an ongoing manner in order for the dog park to operate correctly.

Signage

Signage is a key factor in the enjoyment and success of a dog park. It is truly a mandatory feature in the facility, and it can actually make or break the dog park experience for all. Remember, too, the important role signage plays in relation to municipal liability. Really, two components are present here: (1) the meaning of the information provided on the signs and (2) the look and structure of the signs themselves.

Signs must be clear, understandable, and easy to read. They must be more than a list of dos and don'ts. They should convey information that is personable and customer-service oriented. The majority of users should feel the rules are fair and reasonable; if not, there will be complaints, arguments, or controversy. Examples here might include concerns about the age of children allowed in the dog park, or users who frequently don't pick up after their dogs. Others may be dissatisfied with the facility's hours of operation and may prefer, say, an earlier daily opening. All these types of concerns, through an evaluation of the dog park, should be noted and addressed, even if those responsible decide not to make any changes.

In relation to the signage structures, the signs should be located in appropriate locations and of appropriate height. The print on them should be of sufficient size. They should be in good condition and structurally sound: not leaning, damaged, faded, or dirty, for examples. If a sign has landscaping around it, which is often the case with the primary signage at the park's main entrance, the plantings should not be overgrown so as to obstruct the signage. Most of these concerns, understandably, relate to basic maintenance. Park facility evaluation should always include assessing the signage, its condition, and its location.

Optional Equipment

Agility equipment, sculptures and art, play pieces, and other types of extras in a dog park should be included along with all other equipment and structures when evaluating the facility. These nonessential items can be easily overlooked in an evaluation. However, they are often in poor condition, and thus should certainly be included. They contribute to the overall appearance of the dog park. If not well maintained, they can create a negative perspective—even though those items were often originally installed in a dog park to *enhance* its look!

The poor condition of this bridge presents a hazard to users and detracts from the park's overall appearance.

Formal Evaluations

The evaluation discussed thus far includes the basic topics that should be included in a comprehensive but informal evaluation of a dog park facility. In other words, this type of evaluation would be considered a nonscientific review of a community dog park that could be conducted by agency staff. In most, but certainly not all, communities, developing an evaluation format based on this information should be sufficient (see the Dog Park Evaluation Form). Municipalities that might be seeking a more formal, scientific-oriented evaluative study should consider hiring professional park consultants who conduct these types of research. Typically, however, these higher-level evaluations may be conducted on an entire park system, often to determine long-term master plans, for example. A dog park might be but one component of such a study, but it could nevertheless provide substantial, helpful information.

Dog Park Evaluation Form

Questions	OK, corrections not needed	Comments	Corrections recommended
Design elements			
Are the design and layout of the dog park working satisfactorily?			
Are there any problem places within, or outside of, the fencing?			
Are there design issues related to visual concerns of users' ability to monitor their dogs?			
Is there adequate parking? If so, is it conveniently located and maintained?			
Any related unanticipated problems?			
Natural features and elements			
Are there any problems with sight lines?			
Are there problems with any trees or shrubs in the park?			
Are there any problems with shade? (Not enough? Too much? In the wrong place?)			
Are features such as rock outcroppings problematic?			
Have natural occurrences such as weather or climate issues caused problems?			

Questions	OK, corrections not needed	Comments	Corrections recommended
Are users expressing concerns about any of the natural features or elements of the dog park?			
Any related unanticipated problems?			
Structural elements			
Are the height, material, and installation of the fencing adequate?			
Have there been any problems with the fencing?			
Are the gates working well?			
Are the hardscape areas maintaining their original condition well?			
Are hardscape repairs needed?			
Are there any maintenance issues with the hardscape areas?			
Any related unanticipated problems?			
Benches			
Are the benches located well? Are they being used?			
Are there enough benches?			
Are the benches in good condition?			
Are users commenting or complaining about the benches?			

> *continued*

Dog Park Evaluation Form > *continued*

Questions	OK, corrections not needed	Comments	Corrections recommended
Fountains			
Are the fountains in good condition and working well (no leaks or puddles)?			
Any concerns or complaints about the fountains from users?			
Waste-bag stations			
Are the waste-bag stations located well? Are they being used properly?			
Are there enough waste-bag stations?			
Are the waste-bag stations in good condition?			
Are the waste-bag stations being replenished regularly or are they often empty?			
Is the type of waste bags satisfactory for dog owners?			
Are the users commenting or complaining about the waste-bag stations?			
Waste cans			
Are the waste cans located well? Are they being used?			

Questions	OK, corrections not needed	Comments	Corrections recommended
Are there enough waste cans?			
Are the waste cans in good condition?			
Are the waste cans being emptied frequently enough?			
Are users commenting or complaining about the waste cans?			
Signage			
Is the signage adequate and well located?			
Have there been any issues with the rules?			
Is additional signage warranted?			
Are the signs large enough and readable?			
Are there enough signs? Too many signs?			
Are the signs in good condition, attractive, and maintained?			
Bulletin board			
Is there some type of bulletin board in the dog park? If so, is it well located, in good condition, and being maintained?			

> *continued*

Dog Park Evaluation Form > *continued*

Questions	OK, corrections not needed	Comments	Corrections recommended
Art or sculpture pieces			
Are there any art or sculpture pieces in the dog park? If so, are they in good condition?			
Agility or playground equipment			
Is there any agility or dog playground equipment in the dog park? If so, is it appropriately located, in good condition, and being maintained?			
Restrooms			
Are there restrooms available for dog park users? If so, are they well located, in good condition, and being maintained?			
Other			
Are there any other problems or concerns?			

From Glasser, M.R. (2013). *Dog park design, development, and operation* (Champaign, IL: Human Kinetics).

In addition to the topics already identified and covered in this chapter, a more formal, scientific approach could yield the following examples of information:

- Number of dog park users
- How and when users access the dog park—this could include modes of transportation, proximity to residents' homes or workplaces, frequency of usage by time of day and day of the week, and length of visits.
- Type of activities most enjoyed at the dog park (reflecting both users and their dogs)
- Features of the dog park that users enjoy or appreciate most
- Degree of satisfaction with the dog park and its amenities
- Level of safety and comfort experienced in the dog park

- Effectiveness of dog park signage
- Maintenance issues and park conditions
- Features that are most and least liked (reflecting possible needs for change)

You can easily see that this type of evaluation could provide considerable additional information, but it also exhibits a good amount of similar information that could be obtained in the simpler, in-house format.

Any evaluation should point out the pluses and minuses of a park facility, but it should also identify where improvements, additions, or issues should be addressed, as well as provide information for future planning and budgeting. The following are examples of information determined from evaluation results:

- More parking is needed.
- ADA access must be improved.
- At least one bench must be relocated.
- Consider providing restrooms near the dog park, even if they are only portable ones for use during the high season.
- In some fashion, more shade is needed in the dog park.
- Particular rules should be altered (if appropriate).
- Waste cans should be emptied more frequently during the high-use season.

These examples of evaluation results and many others are typical in that they indicate ways to make a dog park more enjoyable, satisfying, desirable, and successful. With all the effort, money, and time taken to develop the dog park facility, everyone involved should want it to be all that was envisioned. So, it should be maintained and periodically tweaked as needed. This is especially necessary within the first few years of operation, as well as if it is the first dog park created in the community. Also, as a new park facility, it should be viewed as an additional asset in a community's park inventory. It may perhaps even be considered a new priority for maintenance, since many community residents may be skeptical of a new park they believe has been designed for dogs (versus dog owners) and may expect otherwise. One would hope they'll be pleasantly surprised at seeing that a dog park can be as attractive and well maintained as the other park facilities throughout their community. Evaluation is always a first step in assuring the community that the powers that be truly care about the dog park and want the residents to be happy and proud of their special facility.

So now we're off to marketing, programming, and, well, fun in the new dog park! We get to tell others about the new terrific facility, its special features, how much they are going to enjoy using it with their beloved pets, and about the fun activities and events that will be offered in the dog park! We'll all be barking up a storm, singing the dog park's praises!

Marketing and Programming

Don't let your dog park be your community's best-kept secret! Find out how to keep interest alive and growing!

Now for the fun stuff—getting the word about the terrific new community dog park out and getting the dogs (and their owners, of course) in the park! This chapter focuses on publicizing and marketing the new facility and using programming and event ideas to highlight opportunities at the park—that is, besides the opportunity for regular visits for everyday off-leash fun and recreation.

Marketing

Basically, a dog park can be marketed the same way as *any* recreation and park facility. Problem is, we seldom market our facilities! We can, but we usually don't. The difference here, especially if the new dog park is the first one developed in the community, is that it is a unique new facility that people are often curious about. If residents are not interested, they can and should be! Thus, marketing the facility to the municipality ought to be a natural progression of its development. Plus, it's a great opportunity to show off the community's cutting edge foresight, its responsiveness to its constituents, and its willingness to create a rather novel park concept that appeals to forward-thinking dog owners in the community. It is, after all, a brand-new park amenity available to all for fun and recreation! The fact that it may be a new concept to many of the residents certainly means you have an opportunity to show them how wonderful the new facility is and how enjoyable it can be for both the dog owners and everyone else!

That said, once the grand opening has been conducted, marketing can become a regular feature in the parks and recreation program brochure, in whatever format they offer—a mailed booklet, a flier, any online informational piece, or a more formal publication distributed through the schools, libraries, and so on. This provides a great start in places where many community members may already be regularly seeking new information. Within any of those types of venues or in other similar locations, include a blurb or photos with descriptions. Of course, throughout the first year or two of the new facility's existence, highlight this info in a special format if possible.

Now, couple the preceding marketing strategies from the grand opening with periodic items in local newspapers, television, and radio, as well as with popular social media like Facebook and Twitter. The more the word gets out about the community's new dog park, the greater the likelihood of its *appropriate* usage (e.g., following the rules), of community enjoyment by both dog owners and spectators, and, as a result, of additional positive publicity.

Speaking of dog park spectators, they can be an important part of the marketing of the park. Not everyone in the community has a dog, but everyone can still enjoy the dog park! Watching dogs play, romp, and have fun in the dog park is very enjoyable for folks; therefore, your publicity should reflect that. Invite people to come on down to check out the new dog park and watch the fun unfold as each dog arrives and joins in with the others in the off-leash enclosure. Encourage them by mentioning it's a whole new way to enjoy their local park! Your marketing can aim at getting folks from all the various neighborhoods in the community interested, curious, and, hopefully, maybe even excited about

Your marketing should show your community that the dog park is a fun, positive place for dogs and people alike.

and proud of the new facility in their municipality. Again, the marketing can create all of this—as well it should!

Notice that the preceding information, as for *any* aspect of a good parks and recreation agency, is all about creating positive feelings about quality of life in a hometown. In this case, it's simply in relation to a particular facility. The facility, instead of relating to sports, picnicking, or a playground, is about people recreating with their pets. Since that concept for dog owners sounds wonderful, so too should it resound in a unique, positive way with others in the community. Thus, let everyone know. Show them how special the new facility is. Don't let it be the secret venue that people come across and say, rather astonished, "I didn't know *this* was here!"

Programming

So what else can we do to market the new dog park? Dog park programs, though not really abundant, like our *regular* programs (for people), are indeed out there. The parks and recreation department may lead the way, but that's not to say that private canine-related groups can't provide program opportunities as well. The parks professionals may encourage programming of all types, since the dog-owning constituents are as varied as the dogs are! The fact is, I've heard recreation professionals say, "If dog-oriented program opportunities are offered, they will come," meaning that people will gladly, almost eagerly, register for those programs, and they'll show up looking forward to a fun experience with their pets. After all, it is often the only show in town they can enjoy *with* their dogs, and they are thrilled and grateful to have that unique, very special opportunity! With that in mind, since you already have the perfect new venue in which to provide those types of opportunities, how could you *not* provide it?

With that introduction, this chapter suggests some programming ideas, followed by some ideas for special events. Keep in mind that, as previously indicated, while the new dog park can certainly provide the appropriate venue for programs, some can be held elsewhere in the community. These may relate to weather, particular types of classes, scheduling, seasonal issues, and so on. If the dog park is to be used for *any* programming, it can usually be accommodated with separate scheduling and signage (e.g., "On Tuesdays in May, May 1–22, the dog park will be closed from 4:00–5:15 p.m. while dog obedience training classes are conducted. Those interested should register as soon as possible! Regular dog park users are asked to plan their visits either before 4:00 p.m. or after 5:15 p.m. on those four Tuesdays."). The fact that the community *has* a dog park, whether programming is held in it or not, still provides the impetus for the new programs and events. Thus, these offerings reflect a new, positive attitude of the importance of pets' contribution to quality of life in the community.

- **Obedience training.** What better program to be offered in a community with a brand new dog park? Quite a variety of different types of obedience courses exist, including for various ages of dogs and for different instructional and ability levels. Instructors offer various types of dog obedience classes. These can include the five basic obedience commands for dogs of *sit, stay, heel, come,* and *down,* through advanced courses involving going off lead, retrieving, and even performing tricks! Some classes may provide training for dogs to learn the skills they need to become therapy dogs, while other programs are geared toward puppies and appropriate manners.

- **Puppy socials.** These programs help puppies learn to socialize, play, and have fun with other dogs. Sometimes, this activity may be initially incorporated with an obedience training course. Basically, puppies play with other puppies, off leash, in a supervised setting. They learn how to communicate better and be more confident with other dogs. As a result, they frequently become better adjusted as adults. The dog park provides a perfect venue for this type of program.

- **Dog camp.** These programs can provide a number of educational components for younger dog owners. Topics can include feeding, care, exercise, training, and an assortment of activities, including learning and following the rules and etiquette of dog parks. The youngsters learn how to be sensible, caring, and responsible pet owners.

- **Agility training.** Agility training is a rapidly growing sport where owners and handlers guide their dogs to correctly and rapidly perform a series of procedures involving a variety of obstacles, such as jumps, tunnels, seesaws, and weave poles. A number of agility organizations throughout the country hold trials where dog and handler teams compete and earn titles. Agility training courses are offered for starters or novices, intermediates, and masters, with increasing difficulty and complexity at each successive level. The sense of fun and teamwork that is developed reflects a very special relationship between dog and owner.

- **Fitness programs.** Personal trainers conduct workouts for owners and their dogs to perform together! The owner focuses on building cardio endurance, strength, flexibility, and muscle tone, while the dogs learn to heel during both walking and jogging. These programs improve the dog's obedience as well as fitness for both owner and dog.

- **"Doga," or yoga with your dog.** This is a fun way for owners to explore yoga, massage, and stretching and relaxation techniques with their dogs. The owner deepens their connection to their dog, learns to bring their dog to a greater level of calm and relaxation, and learns the basic principles of yoga, including benefits for themselves and their dog.

- **American Red Cross Pet First Aid.** The American Red Cross, a well known and well respected organization, offers this pet-oriented hands-on course to provide pet owners with both the skills and confidence necessary to tend to unexpected emergencies until they can get their pet to a veterinarian. The related program manuals teach pet owners how to recognize an emergency, administer medications, perform first aid and CPR, treat common problems and emergencies requiring immediate attention, and stock a first aid kit for

What better place for puppies to learn and practice social skills than in a community dog park?

pets. It also addresses urgent care situations, such as car accidents, wounds, electric shock, and eye, foot, and ear injuries.

• **Pet photography.** This course enables owners to take better photos of their pets and to have fun doing so. It provides a pet-oriented look at the basics of camera equipment, lighting, and composition, and then addresses a variety of specific pet-photography challenges.

• **Social events.** Yappy hours, dog day afternoons, dog-themed movies, and even make-your-own-dog-toy classes are wonderful ways to encourage dog park usage.

Special Events

Now, let's clarify the difference between special events and programs. Special events are usually one-time or short-term activities, often held annually, while programs encompass multiple sessions or meetings over a period of time. They may even be ongoing throughout the year. For example, an event, such as a Halloween costume contest for dogs, might be held as part of a parks and recreation department's one-time Halloween extravaganza event for families. It may also be an annual October community event held in the dog park. In

A pet parade (with or without costumes) is a popular and festive way to celebrate a community's new dog park!

contrast, a program, such as a dog obedience class, may be held once per week for a period of eight weeks.

As previously mentioned in the program section, the dog park would be an appropriate venue location for most of the events here, but perhaps not all. In some cases, the location might be near the dog park, but not actually in it. A parade route might go down Main Street and end in the dog park. It might be easier and might make more sense to conduct a dog wash in a parking area or in an enclosed space near restrooms or another water source than to use the dog park and possibly render it muddy or messy for days. Common sense must apply here, but again, most of the activities listed could indeed use the dog park itself.

For some events, portable bleachers may be placed along the outside of the dog park's fenced enclosures to encourage spectator attendance. As long as they can be safely secured, attendees can comfortably sit to watch the goings-on rather than standing or leaning along the fence or watching through the fencing from portable seating. Accommodating spectators, in addition to the dog owners and their dogs, in this fashion encourages even more participation and facilitates fun for everyone.

Though some events and contests are addressed in the grand opening chapter, many other types of dog-related events are fun and worthwhile for the dog-owning constituents of any community. I suggest some here, but, with a little creative thinking, recreation staff can develop new, unique event ideas for owners and families to enjoy with their canine pets. Don't forget to also have fun developing creative, interesting, fun names and titles for the events.

- **Dog art show.** Residents of all ages can enter artwork they've created depicting their pets. Any media can be accepted. If the show is actually a contest, many categories can be created. Folks love this opportunity to creatively draw, paint, or sculpt their dogs, and others truly enjoy seeing the artwork. I've seen entire school classes create a mural, where each student contributes their own creation, ultimately producing a huge, colorful array of dogs of all types, shapes, and sizes.

- **Costume events.** These may be connected to holidays or any special occasion. Certainly a Halloween costume contest (or a Howl-oween costume contest) comes to mind, but an Easter bonnet contest could also be fun. Owners can often be very creative, producing elaborate outfits for their dogs. As long as the dogs aren't miserable, since some may not enjoy uncomfortable getups, these can be huge, smile-producing events that most folks love.

- **Parades.** A Paws on Parade or Pooch Parade event is always a favorite. Whether combined with costumes or not, people love to be a part of a parade. Letting their dogs be the stars is a treat for all. Common sense must prevail here, however. On a summer day, the pavement may be very hot, so owners should be cautious of their dogs' paws and water must be available for the dogs. Leashes are a must, and owners should pick up after their dogs as needed.

- **Talent contests.** Though this may be a feature of a larger-scale event, these can be great fun. Whether in the venue of David Letterman's stupid pet tricks or just as simple interesting activities a dog can do that their family likes to show off, people love to watch. They often laugh and thoroughly enjoy these events.

- **Hunts.** Similar to a children's Easter egg or spring egg hunt, a bone hunt that is perhaps connected to a spring event, or maybe a Halloween boneyard hunt, these can be great fun for dogs and their families. Dog biscuits are typically hidden. Some may call the event a real bone-anza!

- **Dog wash or nail clipping.** These grooming activities, though perhaps not quite as much fun as other events, can make for a helpful, appreciated activity, often as part of a multifeature, pet-oriented program. Other services might also be offered, such as microchipping of pets, which would require a qualified veterinarian. These services are often offered and used as fundraising activities, and they are usually very well received by members of the dog-owning community, especially if funds are needed to build a dog park.

- **Pet portraits.** Though pet photography instruction was previously mentioned, offering photos of dogs, especially taken by a professional photographer, is another event that families enjoy and often appreciate. Again, this service can work wonderfully as a fundraiser. In addition, it may also be an event connected to a holiday or other celebration as a special feature. Photos with Santa Claws would be an example here. Even if provided with amateur photographers, spectators may enjoy the process involved in attempting to pose the dogs; thus, watching the procedure may provide some added fun.

- **Dog birthday parties.** These have become very popular. In some cases, they may be quite extravagant. Many types of dog-party supplies are now readily available: cake recipes, party favors, formal invitations, dog-shaped balloons, hats, tableware, and other decorations. Some additional party ideas should be mentioned here, including showers for a new addition to a family (whether a puppy or an older adopted dog), graduation parties (from obedience school), and even Bark Mitzvahs. Numerous resources also exist in which owners can find all sorts of additional information about hosting dog parties, such as games and activities, planning, foods to serve, music, and gift ideas.

- **Pet appreciation day or weekend.** This is typically a multifeatured community event that may incorporate numerous dog-oriented activities, including some of the ones previously mentioned. An array of different offerings, such as parades, games, and contests, encourage owners to bring the family dog out to join in the fun. Often, local vendors get involved as sponsors, and the event may then be likened to some of the features discussed earlier for the grand opening of a dog park. After all, a day to think about how much we appreciate our pets should indeed be a celebration as well!

- **Blessing of the animals.** This is a popular annual event in many communities. It is usually an interfaith service for all ages and for all animals—not just pets. Clergy members from a variety of places of worship bless each animal and often recite prayers for the pets. The blessing of animals has been celebrated for centuries. Since Francis of Assisi is known as the patron saint of animals and the environment, his teachings are celebrated as a main theme of the event. The program typically honors the contributions that animals make to our quality of life; pet owners are encouraged to realize and appreciate the positive connections our pets have to our physical and emotional well-being. The event celebrates how special our pets are, and families who participate find the event to be unique and very moving.

Your new dog park, now up and running, should be monitored periodically to happily and efficiently preserve its value and the appreciation of the users and the community. How fortunate your community is to have such a facility. Don't take that attitude for granted! Care for the dog park with the same concern required for any well-maintained park venue. Your dog park should indeed reflect the care and gratitude of a community that is pleased with a very special place they are proud to use, support, and enjoy for years to come. *Come! Stay! Good dog!*

References

Allen, L. (2007). *Dog parks: Benefits and liabilities*. Unpublished paper, University of Pennsylvania.

American Human Association. (2013). *FACTS: Pet ownership*. www.aspca.org/about-us/faq/pet-statistics.aspx.

Cat Channel. (2009). *How pets benefit human health*. www.catchannel.com/news/2009/09/21/how-pets-benefit-human-health.aspx.

Dog Park Turf. (2009). *Dog goes*. www.doggoes.com/articles/dog-park-turf.

Gelbach, C. (2013, April). Barks and recreation. *Recreation Management*, 24-29.

Guerrero, D.L. (2009). Pet travel statistics and pet travel trends. *Ark animals*. www.arkanimals.com/ark/pets_travel_statistics_trends.html.

Hickes, J. (1995). *Planning parks for pets*. Arlington, Virginia: National Recreation and Park Association Printing Office.

Humane Society of the United States. (2008). *U.S. pet ownership statistics*. www.humanesociety.org/issues/pet_overpopulation/facts/pet_ownership_statistics.html.

Lederer, R. (2009a). *Looking at language: In praise of dogs*. www.verbivore.com/adven.htm.

Lederer, R. (2009b). *A treasury for dog lovers*. New York: Howard Books.

Miller, P. (2006). Dog park etiquette. *The whole dog journal*. www.whole-dog-journal.com/issues/9_9/features/Dog_Parks_15838-1.html.

North American Pet Health Insurance Association.

Pet statistics. (2009). *ASPCA*. www.aspca.org/about-us/faq/pet-statistics.aspx.

Phillips, Kenneth M. (2013). *Dog bite law: Solutions for victims, lawyers, canine professionals and dog owners*. www.dogbitelaw.com/.

Smith, C.S. (2007). *Visiting the dog park: Having fun, staying safe*. Wenatchee, WA: Dogwise.

Wolfe, L. (2009). Pet products and services businesses serve a lucrative industry. Women in Business (About.com). http://womeninbusiness.about.com/od/businessopportunities/a/petprod-service.htm.

Index

About the Author

Marilynn R. Glasser, EdD, CPRP, CPSI, is an adjunct assistant professor at Herbert H. Lehman College in Bronx, New York, and has more than 30 years of experience teaching recreation, parks, and leisure services courses. She received her master's degree in community and outdoor recreation from Springfield College and her doctorate in recreation services and resource management from New York University. Dr. Glasser is a certified park and recreation professional, playground safety inspector, and early childhood outdoor play inspector. She also has New York State public school teacher permanent certification.

Daniel Stockfield, DSP Gallery, Inc.

She is a longtime member of the National Recreation and Park Association, the New York State Recreation and Park Society, and the Westchester Recreation and Park Society; she has earned numerous professional awards and certificates from these organizations. Dr. Glasser worked in municipal recreation and parks administration from 1977 to 2005.

Dr. Glasser is the president of Parks and Pastimes, Inc., a recreation, park, and leisure services consulting firm specializing in dog parks, playground safety, and education and training. She has been a speaker on a variety of professional topics at local, state, and national association conferences and has authored numerous articles for professional publications. Dr. Glasser conducts playground safety supervision training programs and high-frequency playground inspection training programs for schools, child care providers, and parks and recreation departments.

In her free time, Dr. Glasser likes to play golf, fish, collect antiques, play guitar, spend time on Cape Cod, and reminisce about the 1950s. She loves animals (particularly dogs and cats), nature, classic automobiles, art deco, and outdoor events such as flea markets, art shows, and concerts.

You'll find other outstanding
recreation resources at
www.HumanKinetics.com

In the U.S. call 1.800.747.4457
Australia 08 8372 0999
Canada. 1.800.465.7301
Europe . . . . .+44 (0) 113 255 5665
New Zealand 0800 222 062